WHY FERENCZI?

Blucher

WHY FERENCZI?

The empathic style in psychoanalysis

Daniel Kupermann

English technical revision by Mariana Toledo
English translation editing by sf@miracleread.com

Why Ferenczi? The empathic style in psychoanalysis

Editora Edgard Blücher Ltda.

Publisher Edgard Blücher
Editor Eduardo Blücher
Editorial coordination Rafael Fulanetti
Production coordination Andressa Lira
Copyediting Marcella de Melo Silva
Designer Thaís Pereira
Proofreading Regiane da Silva Miyashiro
Cover Laércio Flenic
Cover image Istockphoto

Blucher

Rua Pedroso Alvarenga, 1245, 4º andar
04531-934 – São Paulo – SP – Brasil
Tel.: 55 11 3078-5366
contato@blucher.com.br
www.blucher.com.br

International Cataloging in Publication Data (CIP)
Angélica Ilacqua CRB-8/7057

Kupermann, Daniel
Why Ferenczi? : the empathic style in psychoanalysis / Daniel Kupermann ; english technical revision by Mariana Toledo ; english translation editing by sf@miracleread.com -- São Paulo : Blucher, 2024.
208 p.

Biography
ISBN 978-85-212-2364-1

1. Psychoanalysis 2. Ferenczi, Sándor, 1873-1933 I. Title II. Toledo, Mariana III. sf@miracleread.com

24-2014 CDD 150.195

To Miguel, Bernardo, and Guilherme,
My sensitive core, the source of all tenderness.

Acknowledgments

This book, originally submitted as a professorship thesis to the Department of Clinical Psychology of the Institute of Psychology of the University of São Paulo,[1] has benefited from multiple sources of influence and inspiration, and friends with whom I had the opportunity to establish genuinely indispensable encounters and to whom I express my gratitude. It is impossible to name them all, and I already regret the inevitable injustices. I hope they are the exception.

I thank my friends at *Terceira Margem* for the holding environment they have provided over the course of all these years: Alfredo Naffah Neto, Eveline Alperovitch, Ignacio Gerber, Luís Claudio Figueiredo, Marianna Schontag, Mauro Meiches, Nelson Ernesto Coelho Júnior, Olga Maria Pires de Camargo, Paulina Rocha, Paulo César de Carvalho Ribeiro, and Patricia Getlinger. I must also express emphatic thanks to many others:

1 It was entitled *Neocatharsis and the sensitive way of working through*. I am grateful for the valuable suggestions from the examining board — Alfredo Naffah Neto, Andrés Antunez, Jô Gondar, Luís Claudio Figueiredo, and Richard Simanke.

– to Chaim Samuel Katz, Eduardo Rozenthal, Ernesto Duvidovich, Helcio Aranha, Isabel Marazina, Joel Birman, Leandro de Lajonquière, Luiz Eduardo Prado de Oliveira, Marion Minerbo, all invariably present;

– to my former advisees, the advisees, and colleagues at psiA - Laboratory for Research and Interventions in Psychoanalysis who participated in various moments of this journey. Special thanks to Alan Osmo, Ana Paula Brancaleone, Bartholomeu de Aguiar Vieira, Denise Salomão Goldfajn, Gustavo Dean-Gomes, Karla Patrícia Holanda Martins, Lizana Dallazen, Luiz Eduardo de Vasconcelos Moreira, Lucas Charafeddine Bulamah, Patricia Mafra de Amorim, Priscila Frehse, Rita Hentz, and Wilson Franco;

– to the colleagues with whom I share the daily life of the Institute of Psychology of the University of São Paulo, especially Andrés Eduardo Aguirre Antúnes, Gilberto Safra, Leopoldo Fulgêncio, Marcia Melo Bertolla, Maria Lívia Moretto, and Marina Ribeiro;

– to the friends who have joined me in the adventure of conducting the Brazilian Sándor Ferenczi Research Group, particularly Adriana Barbosa Pereira, Auterives Maciel Jr., Cassandra Pereira França, Eugênio Canesin Dal Molin, Fabio Belo, Felicia Knobloch, Jô Gondar, Julio Verztman, Paula Peron, Renato Mezan, and Teresa Pinheiro;

– to my friends in the International Sándor Ferenczi Network, especially Carlo Bonomi, Elena Adam, Antal Bókay, Franco Borgogno, Marco Conci, Oscar Elvira, Giselle Galdi, Gianni Guasto, Adrienne Harris, Endre Koritar, Luís Martin Cabré, Judit Mészaros, Peter Rudnytsky, and Judit Szécács-Weisz who, with their many invitations to publish my texts in foreign journals and to take part in international events, encouraged me to translate this book into English;

– to Rémi Violland, for providing the drawings from *Maryan's Notebooks;*

– and to Adriano Zago, publisher at Zagodoni, where I coordinate the *Great Psychoanalysts* collection.

This work has received the support of CNPq — Brazil's National Council for Scientific and Technological Development.

Content

Introduction

The mentally ill person has a keen eye for the insanity of mankind.

(Ferenczi, 1932/1988, p. 19)

Sándor Ferenczi is a psychoanalyst whose writings tend to inspire contrasting affects. The creator of the notion of a narcissistic split of the self is one of those authors that people either love or hate at first sight. His personal and often provocative style tends to make it hard to read him in an indifferent, entirely rational way — creating something of an obstacle to attempting an account of his career. If we try to do this by using only our minds, we risk being unfair, making his clinical-theoretical adventure seem pointless. And if we try using only the heart, we may write something that looks more like a glossy marketing brochure, but not a critical reflection of his work — in which heights of brilliance combine with occasional clear excesses. I have chosen to alternate between the paths of intellectual and emotional encounter with his thinking. I hope to do justice to Ferenczi without requiring the reader to adhere uncritically to any particular position, since I imagine readers will in practice be seeking not only information, but above all promising directions to take in the problems they encounter daily in their clinical practice. Not forgetting that any sound clinical solution comes from a combination of the mind and the heart.

I could justify my research interest by listing the various terms of praise received by Sándor Ferenczi both during his lifetime and after his death. It is true that praise often barely disguises an attempt at demeaning by criticism — but in the case of Ferenczi, the *enfant terrible* of psychoanalysis (a typically ambivalent title, which he in fact rather liked), some of the praise was seeking, on the contrary, to repair his widespread reputation in the psychoanalytic *milieu* as an "exotic" clinician, which had resulted from the *furor sanandi* in his conduct of analyses, and from the mental illness that some alleged was affecting him late in life.

On Ferenczi's fiftieth birthday, before he was shunned by the psychoanalytic establishment, Freud (1923/1961, p. 267–269) celebrated the "long, intimate and hitherto untroubled friendship" between the two since their first meeting in 1908, and described him as a "master" known for his "originality", his "wealth of ideas" and his "command over a well-directed scientific imagination". For over twenty years, Ferenczi was Freud's primary interlocutor, his "paladin, and secret grand vizier" (Sabourin, 1988, p. 2). In his obituary of Ferenczi, Freud once again underlined Ferenczi's talent by saying that he had made "all analysts into his pupils" (Freud, 1933/1964a, p. 228).

Ferenczi was, indeed, the analyst of Melanie Klein, Ernest Jones, Alice and Michael Balint, Geza Róheim, and other clinicians who stood out in the psychoanalytic field, but it was in the field of ideas that he exercised a clear ascendancy over future generations. Winnicott, commenting on his influences, stated: "It is quite possible for me to have got this original idea of mine about the antisocial tendency and hope [...]. I never know what I've got out of glancing at Ferenczi, for instance [...]" (1967/2018, p. 579). Jacques Lacan mentions him on several occasions, emphasizing that, despite his "theoretical extravagance", he was the "most authentic explorer of the analyst's therapeutic responsibility" (1966/2006b, p. 192), and the one who "most relevantly raised the question of what is required of the analyst as a person, in particular as regards the end of the treatment" (1955/2006b, p. 282). More recently, André Green, while also making some strong criticism of Ferenczi, stated that his role was decisive for psychoanalytic reflection on countertransference, stating that in this aspect Ferenczi is "a visionary and precursor of the entire field of contemporary analysis" (2005, p. 21).

Since the early 1930s, however, Ferenczi had been the target of *Todschweigen*, the "death by silence" usually imposed on dissidents by representatives of mainstream psychoanalytic thinking (Rachman, 1999). The version that prevailed, which was later disseminated by Jones (1989) in his famous biography of Freud, was that Ferenczi spent the final years of his life — during which he produced his most original and heterodox work — affected by psychic disturbances caused by the illness that killed him, pernicious anemia. His writings were no longer being translated, and his ideas were banned from psychoanalytic training institutes. From 1940 to 1980, his work was unknown to psychoanalysts of the new generations: Ferenczi's name was hardly ever mentioned.

A "renaissance" movement for Ferenczi's work began in the 1980s (Berman, 1996; Bonomi, 1998).[1] Not only were his writings translated into several languages, but some prominent publications started a movement to reestablish his importance, particularly for reflection on the impasses encountered by contemporary psychoanalysis in the treatment of severe patients, who demand a sensitive presence from the psychoanalyst so that the affective encounter can reach their split nuclei.

Giselle Galdi (1996) humorously highlights that one of the discomforts caused by Ferenczi's thinking comes from the indication that, in clinical

1 We highlight the publication, in the United States, of the book *The Legacy of Sándor Ferenczi*, edited by Professors Lewis Aron and Adrienne Harris (Aron & Harris, 1993) at The New School for Social Research, as a milestone for the movement.

practice, the psychoanalyst needs to make himself available to be affected and to undergo changes in his own psyche, as opposed to being a "Teflon analyst" — averse to any affective contact, and with a surface to which nothing adheres — a paradigm that prevailed for a long time while the interpretive style predominated in 20th-century psychoanalysis. Franco Borgogno (2015), also having recourse to *Witz*, parodies the 1908 essay[2] noting that Ferenczi inaugurated an empathic clinical style responsible for the emergence of the "introjective analyst": one who adapts to each analysand's own time, rhythm, and unique modes of expression, avoiding the *premature ejaculation of interpretation.*

But what was so challenging in Ferenczi's formulations that some analysts might have to resort to the playful to make their readers sensitive enough to be able to consider his contributions?

In referring to adults' resistance to listening to the testimony of traumatized children, Ferenczi refers to their tendency to react with a "deadly silence",[3] through which

> *the child's faint references are ignored or even rejected as incongruous, with the unanimous concurrence of those around him, and with such consistency that the child has to give up and cannot maintain its own judgment. (1932/1988, p. 25 [January 31, 1932])*

Was Ferenczi really the inconvenient *enfant terrible* of the early days of the Freudian adventure to deserve the "death by silence" (*Todschweigen*) imposed by the psychoanalytic community, due to ideas that sounded traumatic to his peers? As Luis Cabré (2017, p. 17) inquires, why was

2 "On the Significance of Premature Ejaculation" (Ferenczi, 1908/1991a).

3 In "On Shock", Ferenczi brings back the idea of a "deadly silence" as the paradigm of the adult's reaction of "apparent incomprehension" to the child's traumatic testimony (1932/1994p, p. 253). Thus, one can imagine the influence of his own deadly silencing on the later development of his trauma theory.

Ferenczi "subjected to such blatant disavowal"? Did he represent a danger, or a threat of disruption, to the psychoanalytic movement?

In Ferenczi's case, we are effectively talking about a "disavowal" that was imposed throughout the entire history of psychoanalysis.

Laplanche (1997) proposes applying the concept of intrapsychic repression to an understanding of how theories can come to be excluded in psychoanalysis. In the psyche of the neurotic, representations are weakened due to their being incompatible with the constitution of the subject's ego; similarly, (goes the analogy) the psychoanalytic "establishment" may repress certain notions and authors. But from time to time the repressed material returns to consciousness, depending on what issues are attracting the attention of psychoanalysts.

The mechanism of repression does not seem to be a sufficient reason, on its own, for Ferenczi having been silenced. It may be more appropriate to resort to his theory, considering this to be an effect of *disavowal* (*Verleugnung*), which emphatically silences the inconvenient version, keeping it split and inaccessible — even inhibiting the compulsion to return of that which has been silenced. As a result of this theoretical and political disavowal, authors inspired by Ferenczi, such as Melanie Klein and Winnicott, very rarely made his influence explicit, or did so only belatedly. Even Michael Balint, who never failed to acknowledge his affiliation to Ferenczi's views, kept his *Clinical Diary* unpublished for decades, before allowing its publication, in 1985 in France. Lacan, in the 1950s, underpinned his work with Ferenczi's questioning of the standard treatment, and of psychoanalytic training, paying the price of the curse on those who break a taboo.[4]

***

4 Lacan was stripped of his title of training analyst in 1963, which led him to leave the International Psychoanalytical Association and found his own School *(cf.* Kupermann, 2014b, Chapter 4).

This book adopts a monographic style, proposing the view that the *Leitmotiv* of Sándor Ferenczi's path as an author was: to offer a theoretical-clinical solution to the problem of the concept of *working-through* (*Dürcharbeitung*) which Freud formulated and presented to the psychoanalytic profession in 1914. In the five chapters of this work, I was obliged to explore — as it were under a magnifying glass — decisive moments in the history of the construction of clinical psychoanalysis, examining in amplified form its impasses, and the clinical reasoning adopted by its two greatest protagonists: Freud and Ferenczi. The initial aim was that this would enable me to find clarifications about the paths taken by psychoanalytic thinking in the first decades of the 20th century, which when transposed to the present would provide fertile guidance for the exercise of today's clinical practice. And while setting out this argument I demonstrate that the formulation, in 1930, of *neocatharsis* as a key component of the clinical style developed by Ferenczi was his main contribution and the result of the intimate dialogue that he established with Freud until the end of his own life. In this aspect, what might have sounded excessively unorthodox to those who are unaware of the full breadth of Ferenczi's thinking is, in reality, the result of unwavering loyalty to the discoveries and issues encountered by Freud throughout his journey.

The first chapter presents readers with the issues that triggered my investigation, demonstrating that as early as in the mid-1910s Freud was faced with difficulties encountered by the psychoanalytic method for the treatment of severe cases — which Ferenczi would soon diagnose as cases of narcissistic splitting, the antecedents of the cases described today as borderline personality, which have challenged psychoanalytic thinking for decades. Relying on two key, representative cases — Freud's analysis of Serguéi Pankejeff, the Wolf Man, and Freud's analysis of Ferenczi himself — I demonstrate the limits of the Freudian clinical reasoning, and even the potential iatrogenic effects of the clinical method based on the triune effect of free association, management of the transference according to the principles of neutrality and abstinence, and interpretation as a privileged instrument of the analytic act.

Had we drawn the route of Ferenczi's travels on a map, its point of departure would have been Vienna, where Ferenczi first met Freud in 1908 and where the treatment of the Wolf Man took place, ending in the summer of 1914, when Freud began writing the essay "Remembering, Repeating, and Working-Through". It would then take us to Budapest, home to the 1918 International Psychoanalytic Congress, in which Freud gave a lecture on the future paths of psychoanalytic therapy, praising Ferenczi's initiatives with the active technique. Lastly, our journey would arrive at Wiesbaden, where the 1932 International Psychoanalytic Congress took place, with Ferenczi delivering his lecture on the traumatic confusion of tongues that definitively sealed his isolation.

Finally, I note that Serguéi Pankejeff and Ferenczi held similar positions on the perpetuation of their transferences with Freud — which shed light on the risks of training analyses, i.e. the analyses of the analysts themselves.

In the second chapter, on the active technique employed by Ferenczi from 1919 to 1926, I demonstrate that his intention in upholding the Freudian principle of abstinence was to prevent the transference neurosis created by the analytic device from becoming a means for the analysand to obtain substitute instinctual satisfactions that would increase their resistance to analysis. I believe that the apex of this period of clinical experimentation is illustrated by what Ferenczi called *activity in the association technique*, as presented in the essay "On Forced Phantasies" (1924/1994h). His idea was that, in cases where an inhibition is unsurmountable, the psychoanalyst would be required to contribute to the emergence of fantasies — especially those referring to negative transference — capable of supporting the progress of the analysis, with a view to its termination.

At this point in Ferenczi's journey, we recognize the boldness that allowed him to progressively distance himself from the dictates of the Freudian technique. However, his differences from Freud were in practice limited to his persistence in pursuing an inevitable problem for clinical psychoanalysis: the end of the analysis. Even though his understanding was intuitive, he believed that the reason for the difficulty in terminating certain patients' treatment was that the configuration of their psychopathology prevented them from letting go of the object to which they were definitively attached — which was represented, in the transference situation, by the analyst. Ferenczi realized that for these analysands, the active technique, instead of favoring their autonomy, caused an even greater adherence to transference. This unexpected effect led him to turn to the issue of trauma, on which I will focus in the third chapter.

On the other hand, what Ferenczi calls the abandonment of the active technique is only a partial movement. First, because the principle of abstinence cannot be disregarded in any analytical journey. And second, "Activity in the Association Technique" paved the way for a greater appreciation of the psychoanalyst's own psychic processes occurring during a session, drawing Ferenczi's attention to countertransference and to the material used by the analyst for constructions in analysis. To illustrate the elements of the active technique that have survived in psychoanalysis today, I conclude the second chapter with a clinical case study presented by Julia Kristeva in her book *New Maladies of the soul* (1995).

The concept of *Verleugnung* — which has usually been translated as *disavowal* — indicates the most sensitive mechanism in relation to a traumatic event and serves as the starting point of my considerations on how Ferenczi perceives the generation of trauma, to which I dedicate the third chapter. I show that his trauma theory posits a succession of events at three crucial moments: the *time of the unspeakable*, in which the child (a symbol of the subject in a state of vulnerability) is faced with the unrepresentable element of the violence they suffered; the *time of testimony*, in which the child seeks the help of a trusted other; and the *time of disavowal*, which concludes the vicious circle and in which recognition by the other, who would be capable of attributing meaning to the experience, is denied.

Of these three, I emphasize that the time of testimony is the one that re-emerges in the clinic through the analysand's repetitions in transference, allowing the psychoanalyst to intervene and the analysand to work through. However, the analyst's lack of sensitivity to moments in which their testimony is indispensable to the analysand may re-create the disavowal, transforming the analytic experience into a new experience of trauma; and by emphasizing the role of the other's disavowal of the traumatic event, Ferenczi shifts the concept of *Verleungnung* (formulated by Freud to describe the mechanism that constitutes perversion) to the relational field, allowing for an extension of the psychoanalytic concept to cover not only *sexual trauma* but also *social* and even *political trauma*.

Further, Ferenczi's subtlety of observation adds the perception that a frequent reason for denial is the inability of the other to bear being confronted with the horror of the traumatic testimony. In this sense, we understand that in parallel to the denial — which happens in a *relational and intersubjective* space — the traumatic event can also cause an *intrapsychic deauthorization* in both the aggressor and the victim.

So as not to find him/herself in isolation *vis-à-vis* the intolerable agony of abandonment, the traumatized subject resorts to an identification with the aggressor, splitting his/her subjectivity into an intelligible part — which is preserved at the cost of traumatic progression — and a numb, sensitive core. In these cases, the clinical challenge is to reach the sensitive dimension of the analysand, which is barely perceptible in their associative flow. Referring to the *Notebooks of Drawings* created during his analytical process by Maryan — an artist who survived Auschwitz — I show how the testimony of disavowal has its own aesthetic, which tends to bring the psychoanalytic setting, even in the treatment of adults, closer to that of child analysis.

In the fourth chapter, taking as reference the trilogy published by Ferenczi in 1928, I present the pillars of his clinical style, inspired by an ethic of care. I posit that he caused a decisive shift in the direction of psychoanalysis through a gesture that I call *the turning point of 1928*, which had consequences in the three aspects that constitute an authorial work in psychoanalysis: in the theory of subjective constitution (and in the psychopathology that corresponds to it), in clinical theory, and in the ethics of psychoanalysis and of the training of analysts. I also demonstrate that the specific clinical treatment required for subjects with narcissism (and perhaps any subject) gives rise to three guiding principles of the ethics of care in psychoanalysis: *hospitality* with the child that inhabits each analysand, *empathy* as a modulating phenomenon of the field of affectation promoted between analyst and analysand, and the *analyst's health*, a condition for the necessary availability of the analyst's sensibility.

In the fifth and final chapter, "Neocatharsis and the Sensitive Way of Working-Through", I resume my initial hypothesis, with the benefit of what I have established in the route taken. I demonstrate how in "The Principle of Relaxation and Neocatharsis" (1930/1994n) Ferenczi returns to the subject of working-through, linking it to what he called the *quantitative* dimension of analysis, referring to the repetition mechanism and the quality of the affective encounter established between analyst and analysand. He identifies the interpretive work as the *qualitative* dimension of the analysis: essential for revealing the topographic aspects of the psyche involved in the composition of the analysand's symptoms, but insufficient to promote the expected subjective change capable of promoting therapeutic effects.

The neocatharsis presented by Ferenczi refers to the repetitions that constitute the *quantitative* dimension of analysis, allied to his understanding of psychic trauma. In the psychoanalytic setting, neocatharsis is manifested through *thalassal regression* and *shared play*, two beacons of the Ferenczian clinical style that offer a pathway to the analysand's split nuclei. In this way, the analytical process favors exercise of the ambivalence necessary to eliminate the tyrannical identification with the incorporated object, a condition for working-through, and the emergence of the analysand's authenticity. Neocatharsis thus acquires, in the final period of Ferenczi's contributions, the status of a proposed solution to the problem of working-through in the analysis, as pointed out by Freud — with considerable hesitation, as I will show — twenty-five years earlier.

It is also worth emphasizing that the Freudian notions in "Constructions in Analysis", an essay written four years after Ferenczi's death, are closely related to Ferenczi's formulations about neocatharsis, especially regarding the importance of the analysand experiencing the feeling of *conviction* concerning the *historical truth* presented by the analyst's constructions.

***

Before the reader ventures through the chapters of this book, I would like to mention the impact of contact with Ferenczi's work on our perception of what psychoanalysis, and a psychoanalyst, can do.

At first glance, the intensity with which Ferenczi believes in the transformative potential of the clinical encounter seems to invite an allusion to an inappropriate, and even perhaps ingenuous, "*furor sanandi*". Like all passions, the *furor sanandi* holds an element of ignorance and another of illusion. Ferenczi's path, however, was enlivened by an ethic of care that preserves the ideal of a cure on its horizon only as an ideal, to keep the flame of the psychoanalyst's sensitive availability burning in each analysis session. As Avello (2013, p. 233) writes, in Ferenczi, the *furor sanandi* is mitigated into an *animus sanandi*, the most appropriate meaning of which is "the availability to care for".

The possibility of accessing the *animus sanandi* connects with something that was revealed to me by a young psychoanalyst whom I know when he first came into contact with Ferenczi's writings: he felt he was more free to analyze. Albeit seemingly simple, the comment is revealing. Identification with the aggressor is not exclusively reserved for analysands who were victims of violence in childhood. It is common currency in every situation in which we are subjected to watchwords that are effective enough to make us submissive. This even includes psychoanalytic training, which in its most regrettable versions promotes a superego incorporation that ultimately blocks the creative gesture of the psychoanalyst, hindering their clinical practice.

I hope the ideas discussed here can affect readers in the same way that Ferenczi's writings affected this young psychoanalyst.

1. Confusion of tongues: Freud, Ferenczi, and Serguéi Pankejeff

Festina lente

(Make haste slowly)

When an encounter ends tragically, it is best to start your account with the end. After twenty-two years of an intense and tumultuous relationship with Freud, a letter written by Ferenczi summarizes virtually all elements involved in the bond between the two psychoanalysts: admiration, friendship, cross-transferences, and resentment. The excerpt from this correspondence reproduced below illustrates the standoffs in the relationship between the two psychoanalysts who were most responsible for the development of psychoanalytic thinking in the second and third decades of the 20th century. Their bond can even be considered a paradigm of the risks faced in relationships between analysts of different generations, particularly if one is analyzed by the other.

I invite the reader to read this revealing passage closely. Ferenczi writes:

> *In the beginning, you were my adored teacher and my unattainable ideal, for whom I harbored the well-known*

> *mixed feelings of a student [...] Unfavorable circumstances did not allow me to bring my analysis to an end. I particularly regret that, in analysis, you failed to discover and abreact the partly transferred negative feelings and fantasies in me [...] A few small facts during our trips together also made me feel a certain embarrassment, in particular the severity with which you corrected my obstinate conduct in the matter of Schreber's book. And I wonder, even now, if mildness and indulgence from the authority figure would not have been more appropriate [...] (Letter from 01/17/1930,* apud *Sabourin, 1988, p. 183)*

It is known that it is impossible to change the beginning, but where there is desire, it is possible to transform the ending. What is Ferenczi's grievance?

First, a lack of analysis. Ferenczi underwent a very brief process of "training" analysis with Freud for a few weeks divided between 1914 and 1916 (Lugrin, 2017). "Foreign" analysts of this first generation of Freud's disciples did not have anyone to analyze them in their hometowns; Ferenczi was the first and most prominent psychoanalytic reference point in Budapest, and naturally wished to acquire knowledge from the creator of psychoanalysis himself. Furthermore, due to the urgency of the services rendered to the psychoanalytic "cause", they did not have the time to devote themselves to a sufficiently long analysis in Vienna.

However, if we consider other passages from either his correspondence with Freud or his *Clinical Diary*, Ferenczi also denounces, not at all subtly, the perpetuation of an authoritarian relationship between Freud and his pupils/analysands, based on a manipulation of power granted by transference. As discussed by many authors (cf. Kupermann, 2014b), the effect of Freud condensing both the figure of the master/father of psychoanalysis and that of his followers' psychoanalyst was that, as a result, there was a tendency for analyses to be never-ending, and for almost the entire generation of pioneers to remain submissive to Freud.

Before exploring more details of the letter transcribed above, we will need to go back in time to clarify the elements at stake in Ferenczi's encounter with the creator of psychoanalysis.

1.1 The Budapest Congress: a red carpet for Ferenczi

Freud's conference "Turnings in the Ways of Psycho-Analytic Therapy" at the Fifth International Psychoanalytic Congress, held in September 1918 in Budapest, was akin to a red carpet being rolled out for Ferenczi. Not precisely because Ferenczi would be elected president of the International Psychoanalytical Association[1] at this congress, but mostly because Freud admits to the "incompleteness" of psychoanalytic knowledge, paving the way for the psychoanalytic community to accept Ferenczi's experimentation with the active technique. "As you know, we have never prided ourselves on the completeness and finality of our knowledge", says Freud in the opening line of his conference (1919[1918]/1955c, p. 159).[2]

Using his trademark genetic style, Freud chose to present the "paths" (*wege*) psychoanalytic therapy was leaning towards — based on the transformations required by clinical impasses — by going back to the foundations of his clinical method. The etymology of "analysis" is "dismemberment", "decomposition". Freud is inspired by chemistry: just as a scientist in a laboratory can break down complex compounds into free molecules, enabling new syntheses, in the psychoanalytic treatment the psychoanalyst breaks down the analysand's psychical functioning into its elementary forms, revealing the instinctual motions at play in the

1 A position he would not maintain for long, given the situation of isolation and political instability in Hungary during the years following the end of World War I.

2 Showing a scientific modesty that has been hard to find in the psychoanalytic field since his death.

composition of their symptom. And just as the chemist has methods to dissolve solutions, the psychoanalyst uses *interpretation* — a privileged tool of the psychoanalytic technique. As such, to psychoanalyze would be equivalent to interpreting — either the instinctual elements that determine the analysands' neuroses, or their resistances to the analytic work itself. The intended effect of a successful interpretation is the release of the libido previously invested in upholding neurotic defenses and symptoms.

According to Freud's argument, there would also be in the psychic apparatus a "compulsion for unification", a characteristic of the ego instance that makes new syntheses occur "automatically and inevitably", not requiring the analyst's intervention (Freud, 1919[1918]/1955c, p. 161). Thus, Freud's blind faith in the capacity of the neurotic's ego to promote binding processes allows him to refute the claims of those who adopt "psychosynthesis" while also reaffirming the effectiveness of the sharpened knife of interpretation.

Insisting on the analogy with chemistry, it will not be difficult to imagine that just as a laboratory is subject to accidents, the psychoanalytic experience carries its own risks. The released libido may choose inadvisable paths, resulting in a cure that is worse than the ailment. Freud gives examples of cases in which, during treatment, analysands become bound to unsatisfying romantic relationships, or even become seriously ill. The only power available to the analyst to try to avoid these premature iatrogenic solutions is granted by transference. The psychoanalyst, as Ferenczi (1909/1994a, p. 39) pointed out years earlier, is a "catalytic ferment [...] [of] affects". Occupying the position of the analysand's privileged object of libidinal investment, he gains influence in his ways of thinking, feeling, and acting, thus being able to inhibit or encourage, through his words, certain choices resulting from libidinal investments. Transference is thus the greatest ally of treatment. However, it can also be the third risk of those demonstrated by Freud: the perpetuation of transference neurosis as substitutive satisfaction for the symptoms, which would render the analyses interminable.

Freud (1919[1918]/1955c, p. 164) indeed warns that "the patient looks for his substitutive satisfactions above all in the treatment itself, in his transference-relationship with the physician; and he may even strive to compensate himself by this means for all the other privations laid upon him".

At this point of the Freudian trajectory, transference presents itself as a true *phármakon*, both medicine and poison, becoming the main challenge of the clinical psychoanalysis as early as in the 1910s, as we will see next with the case of the Wolf Man. That is why Freud reiterates that the "basic principle" of the analytic technique is the principle of abstinence: "Analytic treatment should be carried through, as far as is possible, under privation — in a state of abstinence". Furthermore, the development of psychoanalysis would point to what Ferenczi, in his paper "Technical Difficulties in an Analysis of Hysteria" (Ferenczi, 1919/1994e, p. 162), has lately termed "'activity' on the part of the analyst". Through this complimentary reference, Freud proclaims, in Budapest of all places, the prominent place that Ferenczi would occupy in the psychoanalytic field.

The Freudian principle of abstinence is based on the idea that the relief of suffering during treatment reduces the "propelling force" — that same suffering caused by neurotic impediments — that led the analysand to seek analysis. Therefore, it would be necessary to prevent the analysand's suffering from ending before the end of the analysis, "cruel though it may sound". But would this, which applies to neurosis, apply to other cases of psychic suffering? After all, Freud confesses that his technique "grew up in the treatment of hysteria and is still directed principally to the cure of the affection" (Freud, 1919[1918]/1955c, p. 163–165).

It was the emergence of "severe" cases, particularly phobias and obsessional neuroses, that called into question the power of *interpretation* in psychoanalysis, evoking the active technique. In certain moments of the treatment, it would be necessary to encourage the phobic patient to face the objects he fears, and encourage the obsessive patient to fight his horror of the act. Regarding severe cases of obsessional neurosis, Freud (1919[1918]/1955c, p. 166) is quite explicit: they may "incline to [...] an interminable protraction of the treatment. Their analysis is always in danger of bringing to light a great deal and changing nothing".

Thus, in his Budapest conference, Freud defended the paths laid out by the active technique for psychoanalytic therapy, reaffirming that a different clinical approach, other than interpretation, would be advisable in many cases. In the following paragraph, he settles any doubts about his openness to new modalities of intervention from the psychoanalyst:

> *But are we to leave it to the patient to deal alone with the resistances we have pointed out to him? Can we give him no other help in this besides the stimulus he gets from the transference? Does it not seem natural that we should help him in another way as well, by putting him into the mental situation most favourable to the solution of the conflict which is our aim? After all, what he can achieve depends, too, on a combination of external circumstances. Should we hesitate to alter this combination by intervening in a suitable manner? I think activity of such a kind on the part of the analysing physician is unobjectionable and entirely justified. (Freud, 1919[1918]/1955c, p. 162)*

Consequently, in the case of the active technique, it was not a matter of exchanging the "pure gold of the analysis" for the "copper of direct suggestion", as was conceived for the psychoanalytic treatment offered in the free clinics that were beginning to come to life in the psychoanalytic movement (Freud, 1919[1918]/1955c, p. 168); it was rather about questioning the method, in the sense of extending it to other conditions of suffering than hysteria.

1.2 The Egyptian curse: the Wolf Man case study

It is worth noting that the inventor of the active technique was Freud himself. In *From the History of an Infantile Neurosis*, published in the same year as the Budapest Congress (although written almost entirely in 1914), Freud presents the case of a young Russian man, the noble Serguéi Constantinovitch Pankejeff, who suffered from a severe obsessional neurosis and, after a few unsuccessful attempts at treatment, arrived in Vienna at the beginning of 1910. In the "introductory remarks" that make up the first chapter of the essay, Freud (1918[1914]/1955b) explains this was a *severe* patient, whose analysis had taken considerable time compared to the standard at the time. "His shrinking from a self-sufficient existence was so great" underlines Freud (1918[1914]/1955b, p. 11), that "as to outweigh all the vexations of his illness".

After three years of analysis, the issue of time, along with the perception that the treatment was stagnant due to Serguéi's transference-resistance, led Freud to experiment with an unprecedented device: establishing a deadline for the end of the analysis — this being the primary resource of the Freudian use of the active technique. "The patient [...] remained [...] unassailably entrenched behind an attitude of *obliging apathy*", Freud writes, adding: "He listened, understood, and remained unapproachable. His unimpeachable intelligence was, as it were, cut off from the instinctual forces which governed his behavior in the few relations of life that remained to him" (Freud, 1918[1914]/1955b, p. 11).

Serguéi was somewhat of a *Teflon analysand*: he did not react to Freud's interpretations with psychic work and was relatively "nontoxic", always docile and even apathetic, unable to express any hostility in transference and presenting a highly reduced "coefficient of friction". Indeed, Freud's description allows us to think of a true *affective numbness* resulting from an intelligence that was "cut off" from the instinctual sphere.

The effect of the "inexorable pressure" of the time limit for the end of the analysis, according to Freud, has made the resistance and fixation on the disease yield and, as he underlines, "in a disproportionately short time the analysis produced all the material which made it possible to clear up his inhibitions and remove his symptoms" (Freud,1918[1914]/1955b, p. 11). In fact, in 1914 Serguéi gave his account of the famous dream of the white silent wolves sitting on the walnut tree branches, which gave his analyst the key to *constructing* the primal scene in which, at the age of one and a half, Serguéi had watched the *a tergo* coitus of his parents.[3]

Further, Freud emphasizes that in the period following the use of the active technique, resistance seemed to have disappeared, and the analysand "gave an impression of lucidity which is usually attainable only in *hypnosis*" (Freud,1918[1914]/1955b, p. 11).[4] Just before the outbreak of World War I, in the summer of 1914, Freud discharged him, considering that "his cure was radical and permanent" (Freud, 1937/1964b, p. 217), and Serguéi returned to Russia.

However, the outcome of this case was not so favorable, at least not for the patient. Shortly before the end of the war, Serguéi returned to Vienna to analyze the remnants of transference. Freud saw him for a few more months before discharging him once again. In the first chapter of "Analysis Terminable and Interminable", Freud reviews the limits of the use of the technique that establishes a deadline for the treatment, indicating that it is a "blackmailing device". If on the one hand, under the "pressure of threat", a portion of the unconscious material becomes accessible, another portion will be retained and become unapproachable by analysis. The decision of whether or not

3 The image of the wolves in the dream was depicted in a drawing made by Serguéi himself in chapter IV of Freud's essay (1918[1914]/1955b, p. 30).

4 I italicize Freud's reference to hypnosis, in an essay published in the late 1910s — although he himself abandoned the practice even before the end of the 19th century. We will return to this subject later.

to employ the active technique would thus be left to the "analyst's tact" (Freud, 1937/1964b, p. 219).

In his memoirs, written in the early 1950s, Serguéi Pankejeff (1981) reports that Freud requested a gift from analysands who continued to be embarrassed by transference at the end of the analysis, believing that this symbolic gesture would reduce the "feelings of gratitude" and "dependency" towards the analyst. Serguéi gave Freud a figurine of an Egyptian female figure. Two decades later, when flipping through a magazine that featured a photograph of his former analyst's office, Serguéi says that he joyfully recognized "his" Egyptian, recollecting that, after the publication of his case, Freud had told him he had become "a part of psychoanalysis"[5] (Pankejeff, 1981, p. 168–169). It seems that Serguéi's gift was not enough to resolve the embarrassment of his transference affects. Conversely, he who became known as Freud's most famous analysand seems to have become identified with the position of a *passive object*, as materialized by the figurine gifted to his analyst.

Inspired by this paradigmatic episode in the history of psychoanalysis, I have previously named the "Egyptian curse" the disastrous fate of analyses that, because of the *analyst's* failure to comply with the principle of abstinence, perpetuate transference, becoming infinite (Kupermann, 2010, 2014a). In these cases, the analyst takes possession of his analysand by extending his narcissism (related to his own person or his work as an analyst), transforming the analytic adventure into a genuinely sadomasochistic experience.

1.3 The clinical problem of working-through

In 1926, on Freud's recommendation, Serguéi began a new analysis with Ruth Mack Brunswick. He had been suffering from a hypochondriacal delusion that manifested itself after a minor surgical intervention on

5 "*Un morceau de psychanalyse*"; the literal translation of the French translation is quite suggestive: *a small part of psychoanalysis.*

his nose, as well as persecutory feelings towards the physicians who assisted him. His situation in Vienna, however, was quite different from that before the war. The Bolshevik revolution of 1917 had seized his family's assets, and his material condition had become quite precarious. Freud even mobilized part of the psychoanalytic community to collect an annual sum to be donated to Serguéi, establishing a form of pension for the patient who, according to Brunswick (1928/1981, p. 271), "had made such a beautiful contribution to the theory of analysis".

The nickname "Wolf Man" is published for the first time in "A Supplement to Freud's 'History of an Infantile Neurosis'", written by Brunswick, who diagnosed a "hypochondriacal paranoia" as having taken over Serguéi after his previous analysis (Brunswick, 1928/1981, p. 302). Brunswick's account includes a series of associations and dreams in which physicians in general (Freud in particular) appear as threatening figures. Furthermore, the analysis is affected by a secret: a piece of jewelry, that belonged to Serguéi's mother and had been recovered. He did not want Freud to find out, for fear of losing his financial aid. The scenario did suggest a paranoiac element, which led Brunswick to state that the patient, who had shown in his previous analysis to be afraid of living alone, was not successful in overcoming his "father fixation", which was updated in transference by having Freud occupy the irreducible position of a substitute father that Serguéi had not been able to let go of (Brunswick, 1928/1981, p. 309)

As such, the Wolf Man case study leaves us at a theoretical-clinical crossroads, in which we are faced with three hypotheses: either (1) Freud or Brunswick were wrong about their diagnosis; or (2) the Wolf Man was the first case of "borderline personality" in the history of psychoanalysis, perceived by Freud as an obsessional neurotic (indeed, a severe case), and by Brunswick as a paranoiac; or (3) the paranoia that had manifested itself in his analysis with Brunswick would have been produced by his experience of analysis with Freud, specifically by the effects on his subjectivity of setting a deadline for the end of the treatment.

A very revealing passage from Brunswick supports the third hypothesis (which, of course, does not exclude the second). This is a courageous critique of the procedure used by Freud with the Wolf Man. She writes: "We can, as analysts, be in full possession of the biographical facts of the illness, but we cannot know to what extent the patient needs to 'rework' (*Durcharbeiten*) their material in order to be cured" (Brunswick, 1928/1981, p. 309). In other words, she believes the pressure of the threat imposed by the time limit would have annulled the Wolf Man's resistance to the investigative work of analysis, providing Freud with access, primarily through the dream of wolves — which seems to have been Serguéi's true gift to Freud — to the unconscious material that allowed him a theoretical understanding of the patient's infantile neurosis. However, the counterpart had been the unscathed preservation of the traumatic nuclei that later produced his psychosis.

***

In the same summer of 1914, shortly after the Wolf Man was discharged, Freud wrote an important essay included in his recommendations on the psychoanalytic technique: "Remembering, Repeating, and Working-Through" (1914/1958c). In it, the creator of the psychoanalytic method presents, for the first time and in detail, the third dimension of the work of analysis: working-through (*Dürcharbeitung*). The text is provocative: after returning to the idea that the exercise of psychoanalysis involves remembering repressed contents and repeating, in transference, that which cannot be remembered, Freud dedicates exactly two paragraphs to the notion of working-through; even so, they are preceded by the following preamble: "I might break off at this point but for the title of this paper, which obliges me to discuss a further point in analytic technique" (p. 155). With this self-ironic comment, Freud leaves no room for doubt: he was finding it difficult to approach the problem of working-through. But what were these difficulties?

Firstly, it can be argued that Freud himself showed some hesitation in relation to the theoretical complexity of the concept of working-through. The paragraphs dedicated to the concept are not very precise, especially considering the usual clarity of his writing. In them, Freud resorts to categories that are not clearly defined in his clinical theory, such as the analyst's "patience" and the "experiencing" analysis. There is also a reference to the patient's "time", which, on the one hand, refers us to the notion of *Nachträglichkeit* (belatedly) — the temporality through which the unconscious acquires meaning for the subject — but on the other hand, in this context, is associated to the time required to go through resistances in analysis, which seems closer to the enigmatic duration required by the work of mourning. Lastly, Freud reinstates the clinical importance of the abreaction of affects, seemingly forgotten since the abandonment of the cathartic method in the 1890s.

On the other hand, it can be assumed that Freud's most significant difficulty concerning the presentation of the concept of working-through resides in the difficulties surrounding countertransference. After all, the essay was written immediately after Serguéi's analysis was completed, in the summer of 1914. Furthermore, his argument points in the opposite direction from the clinical strategy that Freud himself adopted. It is worth following it step by step: Freud had understood that there had been no progress in the treatment because of Serguéi's resistance, who had become *entrenched* behind an attitude of obliging apathy. In "Remembering, Repeating, and Working-Through", we read:

> *I have often been asked to advise upon cases in which the doctor complained that he had pointed out his resistance to the patient and that nevertheless no change had set in [...] The* treatment seemed to make no headway. *This gloomy foreboding* always *proved mistaken. [...] The analyst had*

> *merely forgotten that giving the resistance a name could not result in its immediate cessation. (1914/1958c, p. 155)*

We seem to be facing a typical case of *do as I say, not as I do*. Due to his assessment that the "treatment seemed to make no headway", Freud used with Serguéi the expedient of setting a time limit for the analysis, believing that the *pressure of a threat* would force the analysand to produce associative material. Once again, in the essay about working-through, he states the exact opposite:

> *One must* allow the patient time *to become more conversant with this resistance with which he has now become acquainted, to work through it, to overcome it, by continuing, in defiance of it, the analytic work according to the fundamental rule of analysis [...] and it is this kind of* experience *which convinces the patient [...]. The doctor has nothing else to do than to wait and let things take their course, a course which cannot be avoided nor always hastened. (Freud, 1914/1958c, p. 155)*

The pressure put on the patient did *hasten* the emergence of unconscious material in his associations, and Serguéi narrated the dream that provided the key to his infantile neurosis (which earned him the nickname of Wolf Man). The treatment ended with Freud considering him cured, but he returned to Vienna shortly after to treat unanalyzed remnants of transference.

A few years later, Brunswick, as his second analyst, diagnosed a paranoia that largely stemmed from the investigative furor that permeated his analysis with Freud, which made her differentiate investigation — "biographical facts of the illness" — from therapeutics: how much the analysand needs to "rework (work through) his material to be able to cure himself". Once again, in "Remembering, Repeating, and Working-Through" we find what seems to be a foreboding of this analysis's failure. Freud writes:

> *This working-through of the resistances may in practice turn out to be an arduous task for the subject of the analysis and a trial of* patience *for the analyst. Nevertheless it is a part of the work which effects the greatest changes in the patient and which distinguishes analytic treatment from any kind of treatment by [the influence of] suggestion. (1914/1958c, p. 155)*

As such, soon after Serguéi's analysis was finished, Freud identified the need to recommend *patience* to analysts. Rather than being mainly a technical principle formalized in metapsychology, the notion of patience seems to evoke the aesthetic dimension of clinical practice, referring to the quality of the affective encounter between analyst and analysand. Patience, therefore, approximates to the category of clinical "tact" — considered by Freud (1910/1957a) as a unique and undefinable gift — which, in turn, inspired Ferenczi in his considerations on empathy (a subject dealt with in Chapter 4).[6]

Freud had finally concluded that the effect of the pressure imposed on the Wolf Man was the cessation of resistances and the emergence, in his associations, of a lucidity equivalent to that obtained by hypnosis. In the last lines of the 1914 essay, he writes that from a theoretical point of view, working-through can be correlated with "the 'abreacting' of the quotas of affect strangulated by repression — an abreaction without which hypnotic treatment remained ineffective" (Freud, 1914/1958c, p. 156).

We understand that the specter of suggestion and hypnosis tends to haunt discussion of Freud's essay insofar as the "technique" used with Serguéi produced "magical" results in terms of investigation but

---

6 We refer the reader to one of the rare writings published in Brazil on the issue of patience in clinical psychoanalysis (Chaves, 2001).

in practice a veritable therapeutic disaster. On the other hand, evoking the concept of *abreaction of affects* in the conclusion of the exposition on working-through is provocative. It all points to the fact that, for Freud, *working-through is to the psychoanalytic method as abreaction was to the cathartic method.*

An analysis that does not allocate the time required for working-through will become a mere intellectual exercise, the result of which will be an analysand who knows a lot, but for whom the acquired knowledge will add nothing of significance to their existential experience. Monique Schneider (1994) points out that, in the history of psychoanalysis, the prominence afforded to affects in Freud's work has faded, leading many analysts to the limited understanding that clinical practice required an intelligible exercise of "becoming aware", with affects being considered an excess to be discharged. However, it is only by working on the affects that the subject in analysis will achieve the recognition of himself that will allow him to "exist differently". In this sense, the abreaction to which Freud referred in 1914 would involve, in Schneider's words, "realizing the affect rather than emptying it out" (Schneider, 1994, p. 50).

Throughout the history of psychoanalysis, though, whenever the interpretive style was given prominence, it could be seen that clinical practice had become an intellectual exercise, through which analysands were unable to use this acquired knowledge other than to endlessly justify their suffering and existential misery. Such a diagnosis did not go unnoticed by Ferenczi. In the entry of January 31st, 1932 in his *Clinical Diary*, entitled "The catharsis gets bogged down, and how to remedy it", Ferenczi (1932/1988, p. 24) states that the repetition of traumatic experiences only favors the analytic work if "something" is added: a sensitive presence on the part of the analyst. He writes: "It appears that patients cannot believe that an *event* really took place [...] if the analyst, as the sole *witness* of the events, persists in his cool, unemotional, and, as patients are fond of stating, purely intellectual attitude [...]". It is worth emphasizing that the *event* Ferenczi refers to is more than a factual event from the past, but rather its repetition in transference. As he puts it, "if we [...] contrive right from the beginning to present the *events* to the patient as memory images that are unreal in the *present*, he may well follow our line of thought but will remain on the intellectual level, without ever attaining the feeling of *conviction*" that constitutes the therapeutic effect of any analysis.

Indeed, in a subtle passage, Freud demonstrates that working-through implies "working *in common with his patient*" (1914/1958c, p. 155); but how should we understand the meaning of a *joint analytical work*?

For Ferenczi, the immediate answer is offered by his conceptualization of empathy, — the analyst's ability to feel within himself the analysand's affective reverberations — the center around which his clinical style was built. Moreover, it is not by chance that in the last chapter of the *Wolf Man* case study Freud admits that "personal peculiarities in the patient and a national character that was foreign to ours made the task of feeling one's way into his mind a laborious one". Serguéi's apparent dissociation between an "agreeable and affable personality" and a "completely unbridled instinctual life", made it, Freud notes, very difficult for him to establish an "overall perspective" (1918[1914]/1955b, p. 104). Following his reasoning, our conclusion from this imbroglio is that the psychoanalyst's *impatience* is fueled precisely by the lack of availability for the exercise of empathy.

The hypothesis that will nourish our argument and which required us to take this detour through Freud's principal essays published between 1914 and 1918 (*a period that coincides with Ferenczi's analysis, and in which Ferenczi is indeed the protagonist*) is that Ferenczi gave Freud another gift (less tangible than an Egyptian figurine), in an attempt to overcome the embarrassments of the transference.

That gift, I argue, was his attempt to solve the problem of working-through. The undertaking consisted of years of experimentation and resulted in a clinical style that inspired all subsequent psychoanalysis, culminating in the conceptualization of neocatharsis, and a guiding light for the paths of psychoanalytic therapy since the mid-twentieth century.[7]

1.4 Freud's counter-argument

In one of his last writings, Freud takes up the accusation made by Ferenczi in their correspondence. His counter-argument is in the second chapter of "Analysis Terminable and Interminable". Without identifying his interlocutor, Freud (1937/1964b, p. 221) refers to an experienced analyst, respected by his peers and with a satisfactory love life who, years later, complains that his analyst had not paid due attention to the negative transference, thus failing to provide him with a complete analysis. Freud's argument rests on three assumptions. First, there would not have been, at the time, any overt manifestation of hostility in the transference situation, and the analyst can only work with material that is present and active. Let us recall the end of his text on the dynamics of transference: "It is impossible to destroy anyone *in absentia* or *in effigie*" (Freud, 1912/1958b, p. 108). Second, even if there were only faint signs of the negative transference, "activating" it — provoking the analysand through an unsympathetic behavior — would be too risky; it would threaten to compromise the treatment's greatest ally: the transference of tender and affectionate feelings addressed to the analyst. Lastly, by making a surprising reference to friendship, Freud (1937/1964b, p. 221) proposes that not everything that happens during and after analysis between analyst and analysand should be considered restricted to transference; there would also be *friendship relationships,* based on reality — not on the unconscious infantile fantasies projected through transference — that "proved to be viable" (Freud, 1937/1964b, p. 222).

7 Neocatharsis will be the topic of our last chapter; we ask the reader for some patience to be convinced of our working hypothesis.

I insist on this debate between Ferenczi and Freud because it unequivocally makes explicit the differences in the clinical conceptualizations found in each of the authors. The mere fact that four years after Ferenczi's death Freud revisited some of the questions that Ferenczi had addressed to him is enough to prove their importance. "Analysis Terminable and Interminable" can be considered the legacy of the difficulties and challenges of clinical psychoanalysis, in which Freud presents and discusses the limits imposed on its progress: alterations in the ego, negative therapeutic reactions, and what he called "the bedrock of castration".

However, had Ferenczi been able to reply (it can perhaps be assumed that he must have turned in his grave when "Analysis Terminable and Interminable" was published), we would undoubtedly encounter a very different understanding of defense mechanisms, the handling of analysis of severely ill patients, resistances, negative transference, the iatrogenic effects of psychoanalysis, and even friendship.

On the question of whether or not the analysand experiences hostile affects in transference, Ferenczi anticipated the answer in "On Forced Phantasies" (1924/1994h). Briefly summarizing his reasoning: the analysand cannot express evidence of negative transference in many clinical situations; due to his subjective configuration, he obeys the imperative of preserving an idealized analyst, effectively barring any access to hostile affects and hate. He also needs evidence to be confident of the "survival" of his analyst and, above all, certainty that there will be no retaliation. In this sense, in relation to Freud's concern that "activating" the negative transference would risk compromising the tender positive transference (the treatment's greatest ally), Ferenczi would respond that the greatest obstacle to the expression of negative transference is the psychoanalyst's resistance to acknowledging it, which would oblige him to offer himself as its recipient, a very uncomfortable task. In the specific case of Ferenczi's analysis, the mixture of positions that Freud occupied in his mind — "adored master", and creator of psychoanalysis interested in the perpetuation of his work by his disciples — would seem to have compromised the transference experience and, consequently, the possibility of Ferenczi carrying his analysis to term. Hence a possible conclusion might be that because in his case the transference was not adequately analyzed, Ferenczi transformed the problem of the end of analyses into one of his theoretical-clinical obsessions.[8]

There seems to be, thus, an uncomfortable similarity between the fates of Ferenczi's analysis and that of the Wolf Man. Both cases show unfinished analyses due to entanglements in transference and countertransference; this was primarily due to Freud's difficulty in acknowledging "negative feelings and fantasies" in the transference of his two analysands. In Serguéi's case, Freud pointed out his "docile indifference" as an obstacle to the progress of analysis, without wondering about hostile affects — which did not go unnoticed by Brunswick — disguised by the patient's presumed amiability. In Ferenczi's case, he believed in a friendship beyond any transference, which was quite convenient for the future of psychoanalysis, but deserving of great suspicion.[9] I do not mean to claim it is impossible for analyst and analysand to establish a friendship. On the contrary, it is not only possible but desirable, as long as it is not mistaken for servile submission.

Furthermore, it can be understood that both analyses serve as paradigms of the gridlocks that would become visible in the psychoanalytic movement decades later, in regard to training analyses (*cf.* Kupermann, 2014b). In the analysis of aspiring psychoanalysts,

---

8 On the other hand, in favor of Freud, one must admit that the first generation of disciples did not have the necessary time to work through their analyses, as previously demonstrated.

9 In commenting on this episode, Michael Balint (1954) does not avoid sarcasm when he says that, in the mid-20th century, any analyst in training would have been severely reprimanded if they told their training analysts they did not recognize any signs of negative transference in an analysis under their responsibility.

especially when there is influence or interference from institutional regulations, implicit or explicit, the analyst of candidates in training occupies a number of positions that can compromise the independence of the transference experience, placing it at the service of the networks of commitment established in institutional life.

The reader may object that Serguéi was not a candidate to become a psychoanalyst and, for this reason, his analysis was not for training, which is true. Nevertheless, his irreducible identification with the position of Freud's most famous patient indicates, in addition to an evident masochistic fixation, a dedication to the psychoanalytic movement that any psychoanalyst might envy. Throughout his life, Serguéi gave interviews to psychoanalysts and non-psychoanalysts and wrote about his analysis with Freud on various occasions (*cf.* Gardiner, 1981).

To strengthen my hypothesis, it is appropriate to provide an account of one of the last episodes in his relationship with Freud. In 1926, years after his analysis, Freud wrote to Serguéi asking for details from the dream of the wolves. Answering his questions, Serguéi added: "I am happy to have been of service to you with this information". In a letter to Muriel Gardiner dated June 11, 1957, he recalls the exchange of correspondence with Freud, saying that the desperate suffering that led him to the second analysis began precisely in June 1926, which leads him to question: "Or is the beginning of 'paranoia' somehow related to Professor Freud's questions?!" (Gardiner, 1981, p. 282).

1.5 Wiesbaden: from the desire to be alone to traumatic isolation

Ferenczi's *Clinical Diary* also contains a reference to the question of friendship at the end of an analysis, which is less surprising, given the context of the discussion, than Freud's take found in "Analysis Terminable and Interminable", but still thought-provoking. Ferenczi

(1932/1988, p. 56) comments that after successive disappointments with adults, children establish friendships among themselves, and raises the question of whether an analysis should indeed end precisely under the auspices of just such a friendship between analyst and analysand.

Friendship would be, in this sense, an encounter governed by a confluence of affects, in which the asymmetry between subjects imposed by social or moral codes — especially that which relates to authority — no longer governs their bond. The figure of the child is omnipresent in Ferenczi's writings and refers to the creative and playful encounter through which new styles of existence can be formed. There are, of course, differences in degrees of knowledge in the analytic pair. However, in true Benjaminian fashion, the acquired "experience" does not offer any prior guarantee for what will be produced in the face of the destabilization caused by the irruption of the unconscious and the dismantling of already established knowledge (Benjamin, 1913/2002). I imagine that this is the meaning of Freud's recommendation that, faced with each new case, the psychoanalyst must free himself of everything he has learned in previous treatments. In the philosophical field, in turn, friendship is described as the refusal of servitude, and liberation from the originally inherited family ties so that an authentic community of love for knowledge between equals in difference can be erected (*cf.* Chaui, 1987).

Interestingly, the speech given by Ferenczi (1911/1991b) at the Nuremberg Congress, on the occasion of the founding of the International Psychoanalytical Association, proposes an utopia in which a grouping of psychoanalysts is able to unite bonds of love with creative freedom.

Almost all the biographical reflections and versions about the history of the psychoanalytic movement conclude that it was after the Wiesbaden Congress of 1932, where Ferenczi gave his famous lecture on the traumatic "Confusion of Tongues between Adults and the Child", that he was definitively shunned by Freud and his peers, ending his days as an outcast.

I believe, on the contrary, that Ferenczi actively sought his solitude, convinced that only a more radical departure from a group that operated according to the principles of servile obedience and its reproduction could provide him with the necessary freedom to think and practice psychoanalysis creatively and, finally, to die in his own way.

It is true that before the Congress, Ferenczi visited Vienna and read his lecture to Freud, who listened to it with "increasing impatience". In the end, Freud warned him that he was walking through "dangerous terrain" and risking a departure from the "traditional techniques" that guide psychoanalytic practice. As they said their goodbyes, Ferenczi held out his hand, and Freud turned his back on him, leaving the room (Fromm *apud* Dean-Gomes, 2019, p. 252).

His theoretical and personal departure was nonetheless interpreted as disobedience, disrespect — and worse, a psychotic symptom; and the consequences were predictable: stigma and isolation. According to Ernst Jones' version found in his greatest work, *The Life and Work of Sigmund Freud*, which has been disseminated since the 1950s, Ferenczi was not only the victim of a serious blood disease (pernicious anemia) but also mentally disturbed, reducing the intellectual quality of his last work at the end of his life (Jones, 1989) — precisely the work in which we can recognize today the independence and originality that turned him into a source of privileged inspiration for many psychoanalysts of the second half of the 20th century.

2. Limits and applicability of the active technique

On opening

Rabbi Schlomo of Karlin said to a man: —
I have no key to open you.
The man shouted: — Then break me open with a nail!
From then on, the Rabbi used to praise this man highly.
(Buber, 1995, p. 321)

Freud certainly had not imagined what Ferenczi would present in "On Forced Phantasies" (1924/1994h) a few years after the Budapest Congress. The re-edition, in psychoanalysis, of the tragic relationships between creator and creature so frequent in human inventions had found, during the time the active technique was employed by Ferenczi, one of its greatest expressions.

I will once more insist on the method of beginning the exposition of the issues at hand by describing the end. The last experiment under the active technique, the "activity in the association technique" (the subtitle of the 1924 article) as Ferenczi named it, reveals the best and worst of this period of contributions to the Freudian clinical method, based on the privilege given to the principle of abstinence in transference. The clinical situation evoked by Ferenczi is quite similar to that reported by Freud about the analysis of the Wolf Man: a very friendly and seemingly collaborative patient whose analysis, however, showed signs of stagnation. After much interpretation, Ferenczi decided to reproduce the Freudian experiment and set a deadline for the end of the treatment, believing that this would awaken the anguish and hostility — in the form of sadism, "rage", and "revenge" — that would allow the analysand to move in the transference situation. His understanding was that the emergence of negative transference, until then absent, could favor the patient's detachment from the objects to which he was attached — of which the analyst would be the main example. Ferenczi writes:

> *one must bring the patient to the point of tolerating the phantasies without onanistic discharge, and thereby make conscious the feelings of distress and painful affects related to them (longing, rage, revenge, etc.) without converting them into hysterical "feelings of tension" (1924/1994h, p. 75).*

Much to his surprise, the patient did not express any anger or hatred, maintaining his posture of recognition and gratitude. Ferenczi then encouraged him to imagine situations in which he expressed hostility — "forcing" his fantasies — from which a scene effectively emerged in which the analysand sexually possessed his analyst. For Ferenczi, this scene enabled the "reconstruction" of his libidinal history by accessing the multiple situations linked to the analysand's Oedipus complex, enabling his treatment to be concluded.

According to Ferenczi, three modalities of fantasy may require the psychoanalyst's activity to gain expression in the analysand's own associations: "1. Positive and negative phantasies of transference; 2. Phantasies recollecting infancy; 3. Onanistic phantasies" (Ferenczi, 1924/1994h, p. 75). Thus it is always about the relationship with primary objects — targets of ambivalence in masturbatory fantasies and childhood memories, and a matrix of affects (desublimated or hostile erotic affects) — updated in the transference.

On the one hand, the formulation of "forced" fantasies points to the limits faced by Ferenczi with the use of the active technique. His goal was to increase, through interdictions and injunctions, the libidinal tension in the transference situation (i.e., to promote the "frustration" recommended by Freud) so as to resume the associative flow of the analysand, which had been stagnant due to the satisfactions experienced through transference-love. However, Ferenczi had come up against the restrictions inherent to the fundamental rule of psychoanalysis: free association. The impossibility of untying the flow of representations from acts that could affect the patient's instinctual impulses led him to go further, transporting the activity to the analysand's own associations, provoking the fantasies that were unable to access his consciousness.

Provoking fantasies would thus imply recognizing that certain analysands would fail on their own — i.e. without the analyst's encouragement — in expressing fantasies of a passionate, erotic, or hostile nature since these would carry the risk of abandonment or retaliation, something effectively unbearable for their fragile subjective configurations. Consequently, Ferenczi's merit in presenting the concept of these forced fantasies was to sensitize the psychoanalytic field to the role of the analyst's own psychic work in the processes of symbolization of affects carrying a traumatic intensity, effectively providing an initial matrix for the conceptions developed by the English school of the use of countertransference for the success of the interpretive enterprise.

2.1 In the name of the principle of abstinence

Freud (1919[1918]/1955c) listed three major risks to psychoanalytic treatment caused by manifestations of the libido released by interpretation: unhappy love connections, organic diseases, and the perpetuation of transference neurosis.[1] It is precisely the latter — which was clearly the most frequent risk — that Ferenczi intended to address with the consequences of the active technique as he imagined them.

In "Technical Difficulties in the Analysis of a Case of Hysteria", Ferenczi (1919/1994e) explores the case of an analysand who had already interrupted treatment twice before and manifested a very similar case of psychical inertia in her third attempt at analysis. She enunciated an amorous discourse addressed to her psychoanalyst, irreducible to any interpretations. At one point, inspired by the analysand's comment that she was experiencing erotic genital sensations during the sessions ("feelings 'down there'" [p. 190]), Ferenczi noticed that the patient was performing a subtle movement with her legs crossed when speaking while lying on the couch, alluding to masturbation. This perception of the analysand's body movements provided Ferenczi with the key to employing the active technique. The amorous speech was indeed accompanied by the masturbatory gesture, characterizing a satisfaction of the drive that she experienced within the transference, which tended to perpetuate itself and neutralize any interpretative effort. In this way, Ferenczi transformed the "risk" pointed out by Freud into a "technical difficulty" that required intervention.

In the name of the principle of abstinence advocated by Freud (1915 [1914]/2017b; 1919[1918]/1955c), Ferenczi prohibited his patient from crossing her legs during the session, believing that this would restore the tension and anguish required for the proper functioning of free association. This indeed occurred for some time, but later on, Ferenczi

1 It should be noted that psychoanalysts have devoted very little time to reflecting on the iatrogenic effects of treatment, with rare exceptions (*cf.* Kupermann, 2014b).

found himself compelled to ban other "symptomatic acts" equivalent to "larval" forms of onanism during the sessions, such as pinching parts of her own body. According to him, these practices tend to become the "hiding places for the libido which has been driven away from its unconscious excitations by the analysis", and the direct discharge into motility would create a resistance that would be difficult to combat since it would spare the analysand the most painful part of the analytical work (Ferenczi, 1919/1994e, p. 193).

The problem posed by Ferenczi concerning masturbatory practices, far from any moral connotation, indicates a sophisticated "economic" reading of the clinical situation, referring to the quantitative dimension of Freudian metapsychology — represented by the effects at stake in the transference scene (*cf.* Birman, 2014b). While "manifest onanism" can be considered a favorable transformation of the libidinal position of certain subjects during treatment, "larval" forms of onanism indicate refuge in unconscious childhood fantasies that should be subjected to the work of analysis. Lastly, Ferenczi points out that, in the reported clinical situation — which operates as a matrix for other situations in which the psychoanalyst is faced with symptomatic acts in the sessions and with the adhesiveness of transference love — he was led "to give up the passive part that the psychoanalyst is accustomed to play in the treatment, which is confined to the hearing and interpretation of the patient's ideas, and had by active interference in the patient's psychic activities to help over dead points in the work of the analysis" (Ferenczi, 1919/1994e, p. 196).

Although some analysts may consider this first example of the active technique described by Ferenczi to be picturesque, the expansion — unprecedented until then — of the range of instruments available to the psychoanalyst to tackle the difficulties encountered in clinical management is undeniable.

On this point, I refer the reader again to Freud's conference at the Budapest Congress, in which he postulated that the analytic technique was not yet complete and was subject to modifications according to the specific needs of each treatment case. As we have observed, at least since the treatment of the Wolf Man, Freud found himself disturbed by cases of severe neurosis, for which the rule of free association had often shown itself to be insufficient. Seeing how the psychoanalytic method had been developed from the treatment of hysteria, Freud recognized that in the face of severe phobias and obsessional neuroses, at some point it would be advisable, in treating phobic patients, to "struggle with their anxiety" (p. 166), encouraging the patient to face the horror of the object of his phobia, and "forcibly to suppress the compulsion of the disease", (p. 166) causing the obsessive analysand to face his horror of the act. Even in cases of severe hysteria, Freud raised the question of whether or not we should leave the analysand to deal alone with the resistances revealed to him, and whether "we (cannot) give him no other help in this besides the stimulus he gets from the transference" (1919[1918]/1955c, p. 162).

It also needs to be recognized that through the questions raised in the context of his speech at the International Congress, Freud sought not only to express his openness to the clinical innovations Ferenczi was experimenting with but also to fight the tendency towards sterilizing dogmatism that had been precociously installed in the psychoanalytic movement. Therefore, it was a political gesture aimed at opening the hearts and minds of psychoanalysts to Ferenczi's contributions to clinical theory. After all, one can imagine the influence, at that moment in the history of psychoanalysis, of the word of the creator of the discipline within the community of analysts. In this sense, Freud (1919[1918]/1955c, p. 161–162) leaves no room for ambiguity: "Developments in our therapy [...] will no doubt proceed along *other lines*; first and foremost, along the one which Ferenczi [...] has lately termed 'activity' on the part of the analyst". "Other lines", in that context, meant modalities of clinical intervention different from the interpretation of the repressed and of resistances (*cf.* Kupermann, 2014a).

Fast-forwarding a few decades in the history of psychoanalysis, the influence of the period during which Ferenczi employed the active technique in the development of the notion of the "analytical act" by Lacan is well-known (*cf.* Freymann, 2009). Still, it is key to bear in mind that the main target of the active technique is the *activity of the analysand*, which is compromised at certain times by symptomatic acts and by the *jouissance* provided by transference-love, as accurately observed by Teresa Pinheiro (1995). In this sense, its use is quite different from the suggestive method and, also, from any attempt to abbreviate analysis. On the contrary: Ferenczi is categorical in stating that the active technique should only be used after the analysis had advanced significantly, as a driver to reach its end, which was so often postponed by analysands (and also, in many situations, by the resistances of the analysts themselves).

Just as, in aviation, we can look at the invention of aircraft as a way of shortening distances (which is still true), but also, and above all, as the possibility of reaching previously inaccessible places; in psychoanalysis the active technique represents the Ferenczian effort to favor the treatment of patients who had been considered untreatable until then, because they did not adapt to the standard procedure. In addition to overcoming and destroying the trenches of resistance, the active technique has resulted in an expansion of the effectiveness of care practices that have characterized psychoanalysis since its inception.

2.2 Taking flight: the work of the affects

In 1920, Ferenczi published "Further Development of the 'Active Technique' in Psycho-Analysis", in which he seeks to clarify a few principles of his therapeutic procedure while also further extending its field of application. Faithful to the greater emphasis that he tended to give to clinical practice than to theory, Ferenczi once again illustrates the use of the active technique by exposing the difficulties encountered in the management of an analysis.

The case was of a musician patient dominated by inhibition, which prevented her from appearing in public, among other phobic and obsessive symptoms, and who had already undergone a previous analysis. Despite having deepened the associative work, his analysis did not have significant effects. In one session, she evoked her relationship with her older sister, who took great pleasure in tyrannizing her, and an obscene folk song her sister used to perform to embarrass her. After much hesitation, the analysand reported the lyrics of the song, becoming silent again. In this context, Ferenczi encouraged her to go further and sing the melody the way her sister did and then to imitate her gestures. At first, the patient resisted, but later, encouraged, she ended up showing off happily, which happened for a few sessions. At a certain point, Ferenczi interrupted the process: "It was no longer a matter of dancing but of getting on with the work" (Ferenczi, 1920/1994f, p. 204).

He reports the effect of this device as "astonishing", and from then on, the analysis was able to proceed favorably, to the point where "presently memories of her early childhood, of which she had never spoken, occurred to her" (Ferenczi, 1920/1994f, p. 204), allowing elucidation of the triggering events of her neurosis.

The first important point in reporting this case is the exploration of the possibilities for the analytic setting to also be a playful and pleasant space, in which the analysand could sing and dance with joy, showing herself to be "a perfect *chanteuse*", staging the same "coquetry of facial play and movement that she had seen in her sister" in the memory of the situation lived in childhood (Ferenczi, 1920/1994f, p. 204). Thus, something that is rarely remembered by commentators from this period of Ferenczian experiments becomes evident: the greatest inspirations for changes in the analytic setting, even during the active technique, were the modifications in the psychoanalytic technique that were being introduced by analysts who were beginning to see children. His proximity to Melanie Klein and Alice Balint, whom he had analyzed, and his declared interest in the work of Anna Freud, made Ferenczi extremely attentive to the changes implemented by these pioneers of child psychoanalysis (Glicenstein, 1992; Halasz, 1992).

A posteriori, it became evident that child analysts, due to the fact that they evoked the traumatic, playful, and affective dimensions of clinical psychoanalysis, had anticipated the style of care that would characterize the maturity of Ferenczi's thinking, under the insignia of *neocatharsis*. Affective manifestations within the setting as a result of the prohibitions or injunctions carried out by the active technique — whether in the form of anger or rage or the form of expressions of playful or exhibitionist joy — can be easily compared to the cathartic experiences of hysteric patients that characterized the beginning of the psychoanalytic adventure in the 19th century.

On the other hand, Ferenczi's conservatism is clear at this point in his journey, as he considered that the "work" of analysis would only occur through free association, with emphasis on remembering, to the detriment of repeating and working-through — something which would undergo decisive changes throughout his theoretical-clinical development. "It was no longer a matter of dancing but of getting on with the work" (Ferenczi, 1920/1994f, p. 204). Nothing could be more faithful to the guiding principles of the Freudian technique, which preferred the principle of abstinence in transference, free association, and the interpretive work of childhood memories. Thus, "where then the task of catharsis ends", writes Ferenczi (1920/1994f, p. 212), "the real work of the 'active' analyst only begins".

However, one must recognize his refined perception that the associative exercise itself can be an instrument of resistance to analysis, leading to an "'misuse of the freedom of association' by means of misleading, futile and side-tracking ideas or phantasies" (Ferenczi, 1920/1994f, p. 207). Precisely for this reason, as seen at the beginning of this chapter, the active technique evolved towards an *activity in the association technique,* which characterized the period of forced fantasies. In other words, Ferenczi never intended to contradict the "fundamental rule", but rather sought to denounce the limits of the use of language in cases where supposedly free associations were captured by the process of the analysand's symptomatic *jouissance*, becoming an obstacle to the work intended by the analysis.

It is therefore evident that, if the catharsis promoted by the injunctions and prohibitions of the active technique collides with the limits of the connection work expected from free association, free association itself collides with the limits of repetition and resistance, both driven by the circuit of affects strangled in their possibilities of expression. To put it differently: Freud abandoned catharsis due to considering it sterile, i.e., due to conceiving it as a mere discharge at the service of a temporary economic relief of anguish in the psychic apparatus. Ferenczi, in turn, seems to intuit that without the cathartic expression inherent to repetitions in analysis — and this does not mean only anguish, since we have seen how the *joy* that pertains to playfulness is also on the horizon of the active technique — the connection work expected from the fundamental rule of psychoanalysis cannot take place.

This is apparently not very new when it comes to clinical practice, as Ferenczi himself admitted in the disconcerting essay "The Further Development of the 'Active Technique' in Psychoanalysis" (1920), written shortly afterwards in collaboration with Otto Rank. In that context, Ferenczi would say, referring to catharsis, that the unconscious "can not be simply remembered at all" — since it has never been felt — "but can only be reproduced [...]" (Ferenczi, 1920/1994f, p. 217). Thus, "therefore, *in the analytic technique, the main role* seems to belong to *repetition and not to remembrance*" [author's emphasis] (Ferenczi, 1920/1994f, p. 227). But how should one understand this praise for repetition, closely associated with catharsis, since "it is not, at all, about limiting oneself to letting affections get lost in the smoke of 'experiences'"? (Ferenczi, 1920/1994f, p. 227).

This is precisely the problem Ferenczi pursues as from the period of the use of the active technique (and which, in a way, I have also pursued throughout the entire argument), which can be described as *the problem of the reciprocity of affect and representation and its clinical consequences*. In other words, how can one extract, with the radicality that the hypothesis requires, the consequences for psychoanalytic praxis of Freud's original metapsychological notion, found in his essays from as early as the 1890s, that every psychic act involves *both* a representational dimension *and* an affective dimension? These are assigned the labels *N* and *Q*, in the nomenclature used in the *Project* (Freud, 1950[1895]/1966b); and *idea* and *quota of affect* or *sum of excitation* in "The Neuropsychoses of Defense" (Freud, 1894/1980a). Thus, if the goal of clinical psychoanalysis is the work of connection within the representational chain, which can be compared to what Freud called symbolization processes, would it also aim at working with the affects linked to what Freud called working-through? And what is the role (the "activity") of the psychoanalyst in accomplishing this?

Returning to the last paragraph of the essay we have been discussing, "Further Development of the 'Active Technique' in Psycho-analysis", we find the origin of the metapsychological reflections that inspire Ferenczi's clinical theory: "The fact that the expressions of emotion or motor actions forced from the patients evoke secondarily memories from the unconscious rests partly on the reciprocity of affect and idea emphasized by Freud in *Traumdeutung*". Ferenczi adds: "The awakening of a memory can — as in catharsis — bring an emotional reaction with it, *but an activity exacted from the patient, or an emotion set at freedom, can equally well expose the repressed ideas associated with the processes*" (1920/1994f, p. 216.

This helps us understand the statement that the main objective of the active technique is to favor repetitions (Ferenczi, 1920/1994f, p. 217). Furthermore, even though Ferenczi was too attached to the prestige accorded by the psychoanalytic thinking of his time to the representational field — which made him consider that repetitions should be interpreted as a means to rebuild repressed memories so as to produce meaning — his main merit with the active technique was to demonstrate the inevitability of repetition, acting-out, and *corporeal manifestations* in the clinic, so that certain psychical contents that were never named could be "re-living" at last, freeing the analysand from their restrictive effects.

Perhaps because the active technique created the first pathways in his thinking for the reinterpretation of the importance of affectivity in the clinic, in the form of neocatharsis, Ferenczi was able to state that "'the end-game' of the analysis is seldom successful without active interferences or tasks respectively that the patient must perform beyond the exact adherence to the fundamental rule" (Ferenczi, 1920/1994f, p. 209).

2.3 The little bird and the falcon: iatrogenics of the active technique

In "Contraindications to the 'Active' Psycho-Analytical Technique" (1925/1994i), written after seven years of experience with the active technique, Ferenczi vents with irony, very much in tune with the Freudian maxim, confessing that the criticisms received were less unpleasant than

> *the extravagant praise of a few young persons [...], for the former were ready to see in this "activity" the dawn of a kind of [...] freedom. This they obviously understood to be no less than that it was no longer necessary to travel the hard road of the ever more complicated analytical theories – a courageous "active" slash could loosen the most difficult therapeutic knot at a stroke (Ferenczi, 1925/1994i, p. 218)*

Indeed, the complexity of clinical phenomena cannot be resolved with the blade of a knife. The cut advocated by the active technique in the form of prohibitions and interdictions with the purpose of increasing anguish in the setting risked compromising positive transference, which is the relational element that, since Freud, was considered the greatest ally of therapy, thus making the analysand's resistances increasingly inflexible. In this sense, Ferenczi is adamant in repeating that "the analysis ought never to begin with active measures" (Ferenczi, 1925/1994i, p. 219).

More than that, he warns that the use of the active technique can often disguise the psychoanalysts' *sadism*, turning the analytic relationship into an "all too true repetition of the parent-child situation", or giving permission for the "sadistic bearing of a schoolmaster" (Ferenczi, 1925/1994i, p. 220).

If Freud (1910/1957a), using the figure of the "wild" psychoanalyst, had already pointed out the violence of interpretation as a risk of the classical technique, Ferenczi underlines among the risks of the active technique the violence (either latent or manifest) of active measures, such as setting a deadline for the end of treatment — "the shock of dismissal" (Ferenczi, 1925/1994i, p. 222), prohibitions or encouragement for symptomatic behavior inside or outside the consulting room, and stimulation of hostile fantasies aimed at the analyst.

On the other hand, his argument resorts to the same imprecise and indeed little valued categories in referring to the psychoanalytic technique raised since Freud's publication of "Remembering, Repeating, and Working-Through", such as the psychoanalyst's "patience" (where making active commands too early is taken as a sign of "impatience"), and the importance of working-through as a factor for therapeutic success. In this sense, the Ferenczian movement is similar to that promoted by Freud when he abandoned the use of hypnosis to uncover traumatic memories: better results are achieved with hard work and patience.

This helps anticipate the 180-degree turn that Ferenczi's clinical thinking will take towards greater *elastic flexibility* of the analytical setting, underlining the fact of his being inspired by clinical psychoanalysis with children. The "freedom of action" of Ferenczi's adult analysands, advocated by one of the branches of the active technique, and encouraging the analyst to adopt a *laisser-faire* attitude, favored the emergence of both the most archaic anxieties and playful "modes of expression", suggesting the creation of a brand-new clinical style. Thus, the main objective of the treatment would be the possibility of the analysand experiencing repetitions and actions capable of providing them with conviction — whether of the traumatic events or of the power of their own self — obtained "experientially", in terms of affect, in the transference (Ferenczi, 1925/1994i, p. 224–230).

Otherwise, the clinical encounter would simply reproduce traumatic events responsible for the suffering of analysands who, in a fragile state, would masochistically offer themselves to the authoritarianism of their analysts. Just like the little trembling bird that, sensing its imminent capture, launches itself towards the falcon's beak, as illustrated by Ferenczi in his *Clinical Diary* (1932/1988, p. 179).

One sees that, even considering its contraindications, one of the irrevocable consequences of Ferenczi's experiments with the active technique is the convocation of the analyst to *take part in* the interaction of affects established by the field of transference. The "active" psychoanalyst becomes the psychoanalyst who is activated in terms of affect through his own working-through of the traumatic intensities to help the analysand, whose connection process has failed, to succeed in performing the work required by his analysis.

2.4 How much of the active technique survives? The Didier case

In *New Maladies of the Soul*, psychoanalyst Julia Kristeva (1995, p. 10–26)[2] presents us with a clinical fragment that eloquently illustrates the impasses of an analysis in which the patient, Didier, has an "inability to represent" and a "phantasmatic inhibition" that make him, according to the author, a "symbolic emblem of contemporary man" (Kristeva, 1995, p. 9–10). He suffered from an agonizing dermatosis, obsessiveness, and a depressive condition that resembled Winnicottian descriptions of the "false self". Simultaneously, the combination of these symptoms and characteristics also makes him a very enlightening example of the "difficult" cases that inspired Ferenczi's thinking.

Didier makes a curious demand to his analyst: "I'm not interested in feelings, I just want to know". The patient has an erudite and polite, though somewhat self-enclosed, discourse. His speech bears the mark of "operational thinking" (as described by authors of the French school of psychosomatics) which, according to Kristeva, was characterized by "emotional separation from his words". We read: "I had a hard time remembering that Didier was 'my patient', since I was completely convinced that he spoke for the sole purpose of ignoring me".

The analysand's interests were limited to masturbation and painting, the latter practiced in a dilettante manner. He described himself as a person with "relationship problems": lonely, unable to love, and distant from people, including his wife. According to his family history, his mother idolized him, and until Didier reached school age, she did his hair and dressed him like a girl. He did not refer to her as "my" or "our" mother (he had an older sister), but "the" mother. He showed his paintings only to her, with whom, according to Kristeva, he had

2 For easier reading and to preserve the fluidity of the text, I will not indicate the page number of the multiple citations used in this section. The interested reader should consult the original text by Julia Kristeva (the passage is indicated here).

established "wordless communication". His mother's death put an end to this arrangement and diminished his pleasure in masturbating. Didier kept his mother's apartment locked, untouched, just as the deceased woman had left it. This seems to have been the triggering event for him to look for an analyst.

Didier was a so-called "difficult" patient, ill-adapted to the fundamental rule, and challenged classical nosography. In the face of this "narcissistic black hole", his analyst chose to emphasize a perverse "organization", through which the analysand remained as his "mother's fetish object". The criteria considered for the diagnosis were the manipulation he would put the analyst through ("we had to play the game according to his rules") and the perception of a lack of connection between instincts and their psychical representatives — language and symbolic functioning. In this sense, Kristeva (1995, p. 16–17) underlines that his pictorial work, as well as his speech, were intended to avoid the recognition of instincts, primarily aggressive ones. Faced with the analyst's attempts at interpretation and construction, Didier responded with polite and sterile indifference, with phrases such as "of course, that's what I was going to say", "exactly, that's what I thought", or "I don't think so".

What matters to us in Kristeva's account (while I am well aware of the risk of oversimplification in evoking a clinical case from another psychoanalyst — it would surely be better for the reader to have access to the original) is the clinical device she invented to make Didier's treatment possible (he immediately reminds us of the transferential attitude of the Wolf Man, with his "obliging apathy"). It is based on her subtle perception that, in contrast to his usual monotonous tone of voice, and the specialized, technical discourse that prevented her from imagining his paintings, when Didier talked about his painting, his voice was cheerful, he blushed and "his emotions would rise to the surface". That was enough to bring out the "countertransferential conviction" that the "*direct* language" employed by the analysand's affectivity and desire referred more to painting than to words. Kristeva writes:

> *we had perhaps been mistaken in restricting the treatment to a consideration of Didier's defensive speech, instead of* also spending time on *the means of expression by which I believe he had encoded his traumas and desires (Kristeva, 1995)*

From then on, at the request of his analyst, Didier started bringing photos of his paintings to the sessions and commenting on them, but without succeeding in including them in his flow of association. At this point, the reader might ask: but isn't that what child analysts have been doing since Klein? Do they not consider their drawings as substitutes for free association, finding in them the material for the interpretation of repressed conflicts and fantasies? However, according to Kristeva, Didier's paintings had a different status from the formations of the unconscious that characterized neurotic constitutions. Consisting of collages and paintings that alluded to the shattering of objects manipulated by the patient, "as if slaughtered", they strongly impacted the analyst due to the "violence of this pictorial 'discourse,'" allowing the analysis to be rid of the "isolating recourse to obsessional speech" and make way for the expression of the analysand's sadistic drives. As the analyst took the place of the dead mother in transference, as the recipient of Didier's images, she dissociated herself from this voyeuristic position by describing to the patient her understanding of each of his "sadistic fantasies", performing a "veritable 'phantasmatic graft'".

In this clinical device that Kristeva created, we can recognize the unequivocal influence of Ferenczi's active technique. For her, Didier's paintings "had replaced" the symbolic relationship between representations of things and representations of words, interweaving meaning and act, and impoverishing his ability to fantasize. In this way, by naming the patient's "buried" and "split" sexual fantasies, inaccessible to associative work, the analyst transmitted her *own* fantasies — evidently evoked by the paintings and by the entire history constructed by the analysis — to Didier, thus establishing an "imaginary and symbolic" contact between analyst and analysand. As the work evolved, the sharing of affects evoked by his paintings allowed the analysand himself to name the unspeakable traumatic element of his subjective experience.

The analyst thus "forced" the analysand's fantasies, by her own working-through of associations evoked by the images brought to the setting, relating them to the patient's life story, his traumas, and his unnamed anxieties. In addition, the analytical space itself becomes inhabited, as in the analysis of children, by elements that are foreign to the fundamental rule, but quite appropriate for the expression and work of the analysand's affects.

As Freud repeats throughout his work, inspired by Haeckel's embryology, what once has been born does not simply disappear. Although Ferenczi has extensively considered and underlined the contraindications of the active technique, it remains a source of inspiration for analysts who dare to tackle the impasses of contemporary clinical practice.

3. *Verleugnung*: disavowal and the relational and social dimensions of trauma

Grattez l'adulte et vous y trouverez l'enfant.[1]

(Ferenczi, 1909/1994a, p. 98)

3.1 Unwelcome children

With the use of the active technique, Ferenczi aimed at what he saw and hit, above all, what he did not see: faced with the experience of the threat of abandonment, traumatized subjectivities latch onto the hostile object just as the prey precipitates its imminent capture by launching itself into the predator's claws. Thus, once subjected to the vehemence of the active technique, the analysand, who already had a fragile narcissistic constitution, will experience the shock of "warning" of separation by reproducing, together with the analyst, the adherence, the bond with which he had been linked to the aggressor.

In "The Unwelcome Child and His Death Instinct", Ferenczi (1929/1994m) uses a few examples of patients with severe psychosomatic symptoms and a history of suicide attempts to illustrate the disturbance

1 "Scratch the adult and you will find the child."

of the "wish to live" in individuals who were "unwelcome guests of the family".

Building on his experience with the difficult cases he treated, Ferenczi conceived an understanding of the links established in the psychic apparatus between the life and death instincts, entirely as related to the nature of the presence of the other/caregiver. For being so close to "individual non-being", the newborn was identified as more susceptible to the machinations of Thanatos, and also dependent on the care that he receives to awaken and increase his "life force", providing him, thus, with the "desire for life". He writes:

> *The "life-force" which rears itself against the difficulties of life has not therefore any great innate strength; and it becomes established only when tactful treatment and upbringing gradually give rise to progressive immunization against physical and psychical injuries (Ferenczi, 1929/1994m, p. 105)*

As far as the forces of Eros are concerned, little is innate, little is spontaneous. From the specific clinical matrix he was dealing with and the failures of the treatments undertaken, Ferenczi acquired the necessary sensitivity to realize that there was a stark difference, in some of his patients, between the anguish caused by the experience of helplessness (*Hilflosigkeit*) that constitutes human subjectivity, as theorized by Freud (1926/1980m), and the morbid states resulting from the "shock" that is responsible for the thought paralysis caused by traumatic abandonment.

From the end of the 1920s onwards, when he began to focus on traumatogenesis and its consequences for psychic suffering, the notion of the *traumatized child* became virtually omnipresent in his thinking, inspiring his most prominent writings in the period: apart from "The Unwelcome Child and His Death Instinct" (mentioned above) from 1929, in the previous year Ferenczi had published "The Adaptation of the Family to the Child" (1928/1994k), and shortly afterward the famous essays in which he deepened the understanding of the mechanism of trauma and its consequences for subjectivity — "Child-Analysis in the Analysis of Adults" (1931/1994o), and "Confusion of Tongues between Adults and the Child" (1933/1994q). In other words, he wrote four important essays in the last five years of his life with titles that refer to the main inspiring figure of his theoretical-clinical reflections: the child who is unable to play, create, and even live, due to traumatic experiences in the relationship with the other/caregiver.

This was a radicalization of the Freudian notion that the child survives in the neurotic individual, and clinical psychoanalysis would, ever since then, be conceived according to the inspiration that *all* analysis is, primarily, the analysis of a child in search of "motives for his subsequent existence" (Ferenczi, 1929/1994m, p. 106).

3.2 The three times of trauma: time of the unspeakable, time of testimony, time of disavowal

The originality of Ferenczi's return to the notion of trauma lies in the composition procedure through which he resituated elements of the two trauma theories formulated by Freud: the seduction theory (Freud, 1896/1980b), and the theory of trauma as an instinctual excess (Freud, 1920/1980j). From the former, Ferenczi extracted the notion that the origin of the traumatic event is an external provocative agent and that the disruptive experience, in fact, takes place at separate times: the original historical event that caused the trauma is re-signified afterward (*nachträglich*). From the latter, he adopted the idea that the traumatizing shock causes the emergence of an unsymbolized instinctual excess, whose unbearable intensity impels the psychic apparatus to attempt an evacuation that, in most cases, takes on a destructive or even deadly dimension.

The way Ferenczi defines the origin of every traumatic experience is suggestive: "An adult and a child love each other" (1933/1994q, p. 161). It is precisely because the aggressor is a privileged object of invested love that the act of violating the child's psychosomatic integrity is potentially pathogenic, having the seemingly paradoxical effect of transforming tender love into tyrannical dependence. We will follow the Ferenczian description of the times of trauma, adopting sexual seduction as the paradigm of the traumatizing incident, but it is worth noting that Ferenczi (1933/1994q, p. 165–166) recognizes two other modalities of traumatic events: "passionate punishment", which implies severe corporal punishment, and "terrorism of suffering", in the form of maternal depression — when the child is held accountable (by himself or by others) for the suffering of the adult who is supposed to care for him, reversing the direction of the practice of care; the latter is a subtler and potentially more adverse way of harming the child's subjective constitution, to which we will return later.[2]

The triggering event of traumatogenesis would be the assault of a child by the loved adult, an act that triggers pain and an excess of unrepresentable excitation, leading the psyche to an attempt at symbolization. I propose referring to this first moment of the traumatic incident as the *time of the unspeakable*.

According to Ferenczi (1933/1994q), overwhelmed by the eruption of traumatic anguish, the child, due to his tendency to symbolization, will seek a "second adult" (p. 163), another adult different from the aggressor, to help him name the unspeakable. The prototype of this gesture towards the other can be considered as the primordial cry that summons the "attention of an experienced person [...] drawn to the child's state", as described by Freud in his "Project for a Scientific Psychology" (1950[1895]/1966b, p. 318). Ferenczi conjectures that,

2 We highlight the fortunate inspiration found in the books by Eugênio Canesin Dal Molin (2016) and Felícia Knobloch (1998) for our reflection on the times of trauma in the Ferenczian theory.

in the case of assault, the mother would offer herself as a privileged figure "for the child to find help there" (1933/1994q, p. 163). However, in the situation described, differently from the Freudian satisfaction experience cycle, this is no longer a mere discharge of excitation (catharsis), but an appeal for the *acknowledgement* of the child's own pain, an attempt to testify, before the sensitive presence of the other, the outrage suffered. I designate the second moment of the traumatic episode, the one in which the child addresses his pain to the other, as the *time of testimony*.

This is a crucial event in the Ferenczian conception, as it is precisely the failure of the *time of testimony* that makes the violence suffered by the child effectively traumatic, taking us to the last stage of traumatogenesis. Ferenczi (1931/1994o) emphasizes that it is the "inappropriate actions and reactions of adults in the patient's childhood in the presence of the effects of traumatic shocks" that consummate the grim circuit of transforming the pain of the unspeakable into traumatic effraction. In his essay "Child-Analysis in the Analysis of Adults", we find a very revealing passage through which the author leaves no room for doubt about his understanding of the peak of traumatogenesis. It reads:

> *Probably the worst way of dealing with such situations is that of* disavowal [Verleugnung] *of their existence — of asserting that nothing has happened and that nothing is hurting the child. Sometimes he is actually beaten or scolded when he manifests traumatic paralysis of thought and movement (Ferenczi, 1931/1994o, p. 479)*

It appears, therefore, that trauma only acquires its effectively destructuring aspect, causing the "psychical shock",[3] with the

---

3 In "On Shock", we read: "The word *Erschütterung* [shock] is derived from *schütten*, i.e., to pour, to become liquid, unsolid — to lose one's own form and to adopt easily and without resistance, an imposed form" (Ferenczi, 1932/1994p, p. 253).

consummation of the *time of disavowal*, i.e., when the person who was expected to validate and signify the assault by acknowledging the pain that took over the child's being effectively abandons him. On the contrary, this third person, who is not the aggressor, disavows the child's version — which is normally only an outline, due to the child's inability to name the unspeakable — or even punishes him for the episode suffered.

On the other hand, as the imprints of the aggression suffered are indelible, it is on the repetition of the *time of testimony* that we act in the clinic, rescuing the trust that was once lost, to give the analysand the opportunity to find a recipient who is capable of listening to their pain and attesting to their dismay. The sequence of Ferenczi's argument is significant:

> *One gets the impression that children get over even severe shocks without amnesia or neurotic consequences, if the mother is at hand with understanding and tenderness and (what is most rare) with complete sincerity (Ferenczi, 1931/19940, p. 138)*

The clinical style developed by Ferenczi for the treatment of traumatized subjects (the object of the next chapters) will be precisely inspired by the offer of a recipient to witness their agony.

3.3 The Ferenczian Verleugnung: *intersubjective disavowal and intrapsychic deauthorization*

The English translation of the quotation from "Child-Analysis in the Analysis of Adults" reads "Probably the worst way of dealing with such situations is that of *denying* their existence". In the original German, though, the term used by Ferenczi (1931, p. 172) is *Verleugnung*,[4]

---

4 "*Das schlimmste ist wohl die Verleugnung*" (Ferenczi, 1931, p. 172).

which I translate as *disavowal*, not *denial*. This excerpt, commented on by several readers of Ferenczi's work, is crucial for understanding his theorization regarding the function and structure of trauma and the production of psychopathological conditions derived from it, and also to support the clinical theory conceived to treat such conditions. The effect caused by what in German is called *Verleugnung* is highlighted as the element that effectively generates intolerable psychic suffering for the subject, often confused with the traumatic event itself. In this sense, its translation into many languages — particularly French[5] — has had the effect of creating separate traditions among psychoanalysts in the real world.

The term *Verleugnung* was often used by Freud in his work as an indication of the defense mechanisms favored by the psychic apparatus, and since the publication of "Fetishism" (1927/1980n) the term has become definitively associated with the resource used by the ego to trigger the *split* promoted by the election of the fetish object; on the one hand, admitting the absence of the penis in the woman, and on the other hand, "denying" the evidence.

According to Hanns (1996, p. 303–313), the German word *verleugnen* maintains as an indispensable characteristic an "ambiguity between truth and lie" that makes it hard to know with certainty whether something is true or false; such ambiguity is often somewhat weakened, in the translation into English, by use of the word *deny*. In his comments, Hanns lists four attributes of Freud's use of the noun *Verleugnung* in its most conceptual sense, i.e., associated with the fetish: (1) the *ambiguity* referred to in the previous paragraph — in the colloquial use of the term there is still a suggestion of "something which might or not be correct"; (2) the *denial of evidence*, and of the perception of something that has been imposed on the subject — especially evidence associated

5 The translation and organization of Ferenczi's works in France, thanks to the initiative of Judith Dupont in the 1980s, played an important role in the movement that has been referred to as the "Ferenczi Renaissance" (*cf.* Rudnytsky, 1996).

with female castration, infantile sexuality, and death; (3) the *denial of representations* — which might be the denial of the subject's tendencies, perceptions or words, but not necessarily the *affects* involved in the situation; and (4) the *psychic effort required* to maintain a "version" that contradicts the perception. The translations most adopted in some languages are *desmentida*, in Spanish, and *déni* and *désaveu* in French. In English, the common translation has been *denial* or *disavowal*.

Luís Claudio Figueiredo (2008) suggests translating the term as *deauthorization* [*desautorização,* in Portuguese], as he understands that in the process of the Freudian *Verleugnung*, it is not a matter of denying or refusing a perception, but of obstructing its inherently procedural and transitive character at the heart of the psychic apparatus, keeping it separate from the rest of the subject's fabric of associations. The perception in question would be acknowledged, but its effectiveness in the production of meaning by the subject would be neutralized, in the fashion of the famous formula proposed by Octave Mannoni (1973) for perversion, "I know, but still..." Figueiredo explains that

> *The effectiveness that a perception is deprived of when it is deauthorized, is its ability to refer back to and engender other perceptions, or to lead, in a given perceptual sequence, to certain conclusions, or even to reactivate certain memories (2008, p. 61)*

The effect of deauthorizing a perception within the psyche would thus generate an "almost-thing" which, as it is not integrated into the associative flow, imposes itself uncontrollably as an extremely vivid memory, causing a permanent state of psychic confusion and pressing threat, which can even become a sensation of panic.

As can be inferred from clinical phenomenology, these are not the same effects as those from the repression mechanism, bringing us closer to the concept of *splitting*. The term "deauthorization" helps to emphasize the dimension of *subjective dispossession* that occurs in those who are in a state of vulnerability. The Greek root *auto* means that which is "of itself", and two of the most compromising effects of traumatic experience on psychic functioning are the undermined conviction in one's own perceptions, and affective numbing, which keep the subject hostage to the versions dictated by the aggressor and also by the one who disavows the report of perpetrated violence.

I would assure the reader, at this point, that this detour through the issue of meanings and possible translations for the word chosen by Ferenczi as the key to his original contribution to the problem of trauma will not be in vain. However, before proceeding, it is necessary to point out that Ferenczi uses the term with a very different scope from that adopted by the creator of psychoanalysis: while Freud describes an intrapsychic defense mechanism, Ferenczi uses the word in a *relational framework*, i.e., the adult elected to be the recipient of the assaulted child's testimony commits the *Verleugnung*[6] of that testimony.

Therefore, one can assume that this is a phenomenon of great complexity, in which the *Verleugnung* is directed both towards *oneself* — after all, as Ferenczi (1933/1994q, p. 163) points out, the adult tends to convince himself that nothing serious occurred (attempts to report the violence suffered by the child are refused by the adult as nonsensical) — and, above all, towards *the victim of the abuse*, with the later consequences of the *Verleugnung* of the traumatic event *(cf.* Mészáros, 2010). In this sense, alongside the intrapsychic *Verleugnungen* — whether within the aggressor or the victim — that I choose to name as *deauthorization*, there is a relational *Verleugnung*, that I will translate as *disavowal*. I also note that the term chosen by Ferenczi, alluding to the term used by Freud years earlier to describe the psychic mechanism of the fetish, suggests that Ferenczi's trauma theory can be extended from the field of sexual perversion to that of social perversion.

---

6 Feminine noun in German.

Consequently, for the purposes of schematization, traumatic *disavowal* is the act performed by the adult on the child who turns to that adult, seeking help to signify the assault imposed by the aggressor. Hence, an intersubjective mechanism. And *deauthorization* refers to the intrapsychic processes experienced both by the adult who disavows — attesting to their impossibility of witnessing the child's manifestation of pain — and by the child victimized by trauma, who begins to doubt his own perceptions.

Based on the above, I consider that the complexity of the phenomenon described by Ferenczi requires us to read the passage from "Child-Analysis in the Analysis of Adults" in all its indiscernibility, embracing its paradoxical dimension. Thus, it must be read both in the active voice — the *Verleugnung* that the adult commits on the child and on himself, deauthorizing the perception of truth in the child's account — and in the passive voice — the *Verleugnung* suffered by the child and committed by the other. But it is also crucial to consider the *Verleugnung* that will occur, as a consequence, in the subject's psyche, *actively* deauthorizing the perceptions linked to the traumatic event.

Furthermore — and at this point, I rely on the evidence offered to us by the accounts we hear daily in our consulting rooms from both actors in the traumatic scene — I do not believe it is appropriate to use the description "conscious subjects in full possession of their mental faculties" in relation to the traumatic incident. One must consider that one of the sources of the *Verleugnung* committed by the adult is the unbearability of facing the pain of a child, with all that this implies in terms of a fracture of idealizations, and even the evocation of assaults suffered in the adult's childhood. One must also consider the effects of *Verleugnung* in the adult himself who, just like the aggressor, suffers from "guilt" and "remorse", leading to the same mitigating reasoning, although not entirely conscious: "It is only a child, he does not know anything, he will forget it all" (Ferenczi, 1933/1994q, p. 163).

As Mészáros (2010, p. 335) emphasizes, defense mechanisms such as "bagatellization/minimization, projection, denial, pretense, etc." come into play in the traumatic event also "on the part of the aggressor". To further clarify our argument, it needs to be borne in mind that in the trauma scene described by Ferenczi, we have not only *one* but *two* adult aggressors: the adult who assaults the child — who Ferenczi (1933/1994q) calls, at times, an infuriated and mad adult, often intoxicated, who does not recognize the dissymmetry between himself and the child — and the second adult, to whom the child went in search of help, who commits the *Verleugnung* by *disavowing* the victim's testimony.

Consequently, all the elements described by Hanns (1996) as characterizing the *Verleugnung* — ambiguity between true and false, denial of evidence and perceptions, and effort to maintain the lie — are present in the Ferenczian scenario, including now the *Verleugnung* suffered by the adult himself and the *Verleugnung* committed by the child in identifying with the guilt and consequently incorporating the version told by the adults involved in the traumatic event.

Thus I suggest adopting the term *disavowal* as a translation for the *Verleugnung* that is imposed in the *relational sphere*, i.e., what happens between the child and the adult who effectively falsifies, denies reality, and denies the perceptions provoked by the child's testimony, transforming the assault event into abandonment, and surrendering the child to agony. On the other hand, I propose the use of the term *deauthorization* for the intrapsychic defensive mechanism stemming from the traumatic incident and appearing in both the victim and the aggressor. Therefore, the effects of the *time of disavowal* are twofold: (i) the *deauthorization* that promotes the narcissistic splitting in the traumatized subject; and (ii) the *deauthorization* that is responsible for the absolute *indifference* of the adult who was formerly trusted by the child, and from whom the child expected to receive care.

In an attempt to definitively clarify to the reader the nomenclature that I will use from now on, I will systematize it as follows: the assault committed by the *aggressor* adult transports the child to the *time of the unspeakable*, the first stage of trauma, which causes traumatic pain/anxiety; the child's gesture toward another reliable adult capable of helping him to symbolize the *pain* caused by the assault characterizes the second stage of the trauma, the *time of testimony*, which is crucial for the trauma to set in; lastly, the *Verleugnung* perpetrated by the *second* adult, which causes the child's testimony to fail, characterizes the *time of disavowal*, completing the vicious circle of traumatogenesis. The child then suffers from unbearable *agony* and resorts to *deauthorization* by *identifying with his aggressor*, thus incorporating guilt for the catastrophe suffered, denying the evidence, and contradicting his own perceptions. As Ferenczi (1933/1994q, p. 162) writes: "When the child recovers from such an attack, he feels enormously confused, in fact, split — innocent and culpable at the same time — and *his confidence in the testimony of his own senses is broken*".

Moreover, the harsh behavior of the adult partner tormented and made angry by his remorse renders the child still more conscious of his guilt and still more ashamed (Ferenczi, 1933/1994q, p. 162). From the discomfort of adults comes the use of *deauthorization* of their own perceptions, which Mészáros (2010) illustrated through the figures of banalization, projection, denial, and pretense, and which Ferenczi exemplified with the following notion: "Oh, it is only a child, he does not know anything, he will forget it all" (1933/1994q, p. 163).

Despite my efforts to unravel Ferenczi's traumatogenesis as much as possible, I do recognize that around the notion of trauma and the ways of saying it, a cloud of ambiguity, imprecision, and even confusion persists — and it did not, indeed, go unnoticed by Ferenczi.

3.4 Katonadolog *and the victim's shame*

A scene from the film *Life is Beautiful* (Benigni, 1997) helps to illustrate the meaning of the Ferenczian notion of the confusion that prevails in the encounter of the languages that characterize the worlds of children and adults, a thesis on which his traumatogenesis is based (Ferenczi, 1933/1994q). This is a tragicomic version of the Nazi concentration camps, directed by Italian actor and comedian Roberto Benigni. In the scene, father and son are together with other newly arrived prisoners in a camp pavilion awaiting events. Suddenly, a Nazi officer enters the place and starts shouting rules in German. According to the film's argument, the father tries to convince his son that it's all just an adventure game and begins to "translate" the officer's shouting as if they were the rules of a playful competition between opposing teams. The officer barks out watchwords; the father translates them as the rules of a children's game but in the same imposing tone. However, and hence the laughable effect of the situation, there is an irreducible disagreement between the content of what the father says in Italian and the rudeness with which the Nazi pronounces his determinations in German; a true confusion of tongues. The viewer is made to laugh by the absurdity of the situation, but it is an embarrassed laughter, and even guilty and ashamed. What do we blame ourselves for, and why are we embarrassed?

We could offhandedly blame it on "second-hand embarrassment": we are embarrassed by the *impotence* of a father who desperately seeks to spare his son from the horrors imposed by a socio-political situation that greatly transcends his paternal powers; a rather fragile father (aided by the slender figure of Benigni) in the face of infinitely more powerful forces (represented by a tall, strong, and virile actor, the Aryan soldier in the scene).

We could also say we feel guilt and embarrassment as a result of an *identification with the aggressor*, i.e., for the atrocities perpetrated by the Nazis against civilians, including the elderly, women, and children; something close to the remorse of the perpetrator of the trauma indicated by Ferenczi. Nevertheless, inspired by Agamben (2008), we can also think of a feeling of embarrassment for identifying with the victim of the outrage — a subtle embarrassment for being the protagonists, albeit passively, of an undignified chapter of human history, which would bring us close to the contrition of the one who, because he cannot bear to acknowledge the version of the assaulted child, becomes deaf and *disavows* the child's testimony. It can be understood, then, that traumatic disavowal is not, in most cases, a conscious or perversely motivated act, but rather a *defense* from being made to witness an abjection that emphasizes the extent of human cruelty, in which the other is reduced to the condition of an object.

As such, considering that our embarrassment when watching the scene created by Benigni demonstrates our tendency to defend ourselves — just like the adult who commits the *Verleugnung* of the testimony of an assaulted child — from the impact of trauma on our subjectivity, we can conceive that the same tends to occur in the societal realm when, in the face of violence committed against vulnerable groups — be it the rape of women, the beating of LGBTQIA+ people, or the killing of refugees — we give way to *indifference* (*cf.* Moraes & Macedo, 2011). Thus, the expression of trauma collides not only with its unrepresentable and unspeakable core, as we fail to find linguistic resources capable of transmitting the traumatic experience — let alone working through its destructive impact — but also with its *inaudible* elements, which tend to desensitize the other to the pleas of those who wish to have their pain witnessed.

An illustration of this tendency is the dream reported by Primo Levi (1988), adding that many prisoners in the concentration camps used to dream something similar: he was at his sister's house in Turin, at the dinner table, and everyone was happily talking. He started telling those people about what he was experiencing at the camp, but they kept on having their prosaic conversations, ignoring him — a true omen of the holocaust negationism that, according to some authors, was one of the reasons for his presumed suicide (*cf.* Barbosa & Kupermann, 2016).

It can therefore be inferred that Roberto Benigni's choice of a style that fluctuates between the comic and the grotesque in the second part of *Life is Beautiful*, using a language capable of surprising and affecting the viewer, was intended to fight people's indifference, and even numbness, towards a topic that had already been extensively explored by 20th-century moviemaking. The attempt to portray a traumatic event always involves an attempt to sensitize the other to the horror experienced by those subjects who saw their ideals of love, trust, and protection fall to the ground.

When commenting on the incomprehension of adults towards the traumatized child, Ferenczi (1932/1994p, p. 253) resorts to the Hungarian expression "*katonadolog*" ("soldiers can bear it") — which adults used to scold children who cried because of pain or suffering — to demonstrate how the child (or the subject in a vulnerable condition) is expected to show "a certain level of heroism" of which children are not yet capable. Alternatively, he adds, "adults react with a *deadly silence* that makes the child as ignorant as he is asked to be". But what is it that would be so difficult to hear after all?

3.5 *Confusion of tongues*

In his essay "Confusion of Tongues between Adults and the Child", Ferenczi (1933/1994q) theorizes about the specificities of the different regimes of sexuality experienced by the adult and the child, providing us with a metapsychological resolution of the structure of a trauma theory that seemed to be redeeming elements of Freud's seduction theory (1896), which Freud himself had abandoned in 1897 and which was buried (for good?) with the assumption of infantile sexuality (*cf.* Freud, 1905/1980f).

Seduction theory established that trauma stemmed from actual sexual abuse of a child by a perverse adult. It was the product of an era in which Freud believed in the biphasic character of sexuality, i.e. that the child was asexual, and posited a second scenario that would take place in puberty, when the latent memory traces of the abuse would be reactivated, now as an intolerable representation on which repression would act. *Studies on Hysteria* (Breuer & Freud, 1893–1895/1955, p. 7) stated that "hysterics suffer mainly from reminiscences" — but in the trauma situation, the memory would be more painful than the sexual assault event itself, impossible to signify at the time.

Freud's case study of *Katharina* is emblematic; she was initially abused by her father, and when she later catches him engaging in a sexual act with her cousin, she represses the following idea: "Now he's doing with her what he wanted to do with me that night and those other times", and falls ill, suffering from hysterical conversions (Breuer & Freud, 1893-1895/1955, p. 131).

However, as a result of his self-analysis, Freud soon begins to doubt the reality of the memories evoked by his patients. In "Screen Memories" (Freud, 1899/1980c), he demonstrates how memory is permeated by desire-filled fantasies, and in a letter from September 21, 1897, to his friend and confidant Wilhelm Fliess, he writes: "I no longer believe in my *neurotica*" (Freud, 1897/1966a, p. 259). At that moment, the Oedipus complex was already imposing itself as a source of the fantasies and conflicts that caused neurosis. In this new understanding, the seduction scenes reported by hysterical patients were interpreted as an expression of Oedipal fantasies manifested through "screen memories". The publication of *Three Essays on the Theory of Sexuality* (Freud, 1905/1980f) is the tombstone laid on a trauma theory that was entirely based on the hypothesis that the child experiences a nonsexual stage of human development.

Because of Freud's theoretical twists, from that moment on little is said about infantile sexual trauma — although his clinical case studies feature the traumatic issue quite prominently, the Wolf Man case being one of them (Freud, 1918[1914]/1955b). How was it possible for Ferenczi to revive the issue of trauma years after the indisputable evidence of infantile sexuality, giving it the prominence it deserved in his psychopathological conception?

Firstly, it can be suggested that Ferenczi (1916/1992b; 1917/1992c) would have encountered the traumatic in his own experience as a physician on the Hungarian front in World War I when he treated soldiers who fell prey to war neuroses — and the clinical facts that he attended to by dedicating himself to the most severe cases, on the limit of neurosis, the so-called "difficult cases", led him first to explore, and then to abdicate from, the active technique. Indeed, the phenomenon of "retraumatization" provoked by the analysis itself — or rather, by the abuse of the principle of abstinence and interpretation — was decisive in sensitizing him to the clinical management of traumatized subjectivities *(cf.* Goldfajn, Martins & Kupermann, 2018). Also, one must not underestimate the influence of the iatrogenic effects of his analysis with Freud, which led him to consider the need to conceive a new clinical style capable of treating the traumatized child present in every analysand, "difficult" or not (as evidenced by the title of the 1931 essay "Child-Analysis in the Analysis of Adults", which might be better translated as "Analysis of the Child Within the Adult").[7]

Treating the child, however, would require adopting a language capable of affecting the child, as the predominantly interpretive style in the psychoanalysis of his time proved to be inefficient. There is no doubt that the child summons a language of its own; even in social life there is a *tender* way of talking to children that differs from the way we talk to adults; there is also a specific way of talking when we are enjoying intimacy with others. Bakhtin (1996) names this speaking modality "family language", which is characterized by the affective proximity and communal experience that characterize the festive occasions that enliven the cultural experience.

According to Anna Verônica Mautner (1996), the inspiration for Ferenczi's formulation of a traumatogenic *confusion of tongues* was the situation in Hungary at the time, in which two languages coexisted:

7 *Kinderanalysen mit Erwachsenen*, in the German original.

German, the "official" language used by government institutions, and Magyar, the language used in intimacy, through which the affects that circulated in effectively significant relationships were expressed, and an exclusive language in which to enjoy the company of family and friends, to fight, laugh, curse, and love.

Ferenczi (1933/1994q) thus differentiates "the tenderness component of infantile eroticism", expressed by the "language of tenderness" from "the passionate component in adult sexuality", expressed by the "language of passion" — assuming an inexorable difference between the stage of tenderness and the stage of passion in the individual's subjective constitution. Confusion arises when adults ignore this structural dissymmetry, by either not giving proper attention to their "way of thinking and speaking to your children" (p. 166) or by mistaking the child's playful fantasies for infantile eroticism, leading to the assault that will result in trauma.

This demonstrates that Ferenczi's traumatogenesis recognizes and acknowledges infantile sexuality, as posited decades earlier by Freud, although he believes that infantile sexuality is not symmetrical to that of the adult — considering "sexuality" to mean the modality of object relation established at each moment of the child's psychical constitution and the development of her sense of reality. In this schema, before being able to experience object-love, the child is subjected to "passive object-love" and dependence on "maternal tenderness". The love game between the child and the adult can evidently take an "erotic form" — the child showing interest in the adult's sexual organs, or role-playing as the spouse of the opposite sex — while remaining "on the level of tenderness" (Ferenczi, 1933/1994q, p. 161).

In the "PostScript" to "Confusion of Tongues between Adults and the Child", Ferenczi clarifies that the adult's passion instills in the child the feeling of guilt typical of adult eroticism, which prematurely transforms the object of tenderness into an object of hatred and love simultaneously, that is, an ambivalent object. According to Ferenczi, ambivalence — which does not exist in the stage of tenderness — and the enigma of guilt and hatred in tender relationships are the elements that carry traumatic potential. “It is hatred”, Ferenczi writes, “[…] that changes him from a spontaneously and innocently playing being into a guilty love-automaton imitating the adult anxiously, self-effacingly” (Ferenczi, 1933/1994q, p. 167).

Thus, if in the Ferenczian mythology of trauma, everything begins with a scene in which an adult and a child love each other — the adult in the register of passion and the child in the register of tenderness, i.e. passive object-love and dependence — one may infer that this love becomes submission if adults cannot listen to the language of infantile tenderness.

It is worth taking a further step in understanding the theory of traumatic confusion of tongues, concerning the fact that Ferenczi names the regimes of infantile and adult sexuality as “languages”. For Ferenczi, language is not only the preferred means of practicing a relationship with the other, but also the most efficient way to influence the other and keep the psyche operating in accordance with the pleasure principle — heir to the “magical-hallucinatory omnipotence” resulting from the experience of satisfaction, and inherent to the first gestures in the relationship with objects in the world (*cf.* Ferenczi 1913/1994d). According to Ferenczi’s description of the “Stages in the Development of the Sense of Reality”, all and any satisfaction would be related to the psychical functioning mode that seeks to restore a state in which the subject keeps his omnipotence pulsating — understanding omnipotence as the feeling that the world is, also and above all, his creation, and not a mere frustrating external imposition. Otherwise, the “malice” of the objects would tend to promote a traumatic rupture in the development of the sense of reality, forcing the child to adapt to a hostile environment and fixating him on one of the “Stages in the Development of the Sense of Reality”, characterizing a traumatic process, with the consequent psychopathological suffering.

So, in the process of subjective constitution, the sequence of stages of the sense of reality is accompanied by ways in which the child preserves the expansive force of the creative gesture: from "magical-hallucinatory omnipotence" to "omnipotence with the help of magic gestures", and from there to the stage of "magical thoughts and words" (I will dive deeper into the "Stages in the Development of the Sense of Reality" in the next chapter). The word would thus be effectively magical since it retains its evocative and even hallucinatory potential. In other words, by influencing the adult caregiver who responds to the child's enunciation, the word makes the object present, transforming reality according to the child's wishes. What Ferenczi calls the "playful satisfaction of tenderness" refers precisely to the fact that the language of tenderness evokes the love game in which the adult acts to satisfy the creative omnipotence of the child who depends on him.

The language of tenderness is, above all, an invitation to a caring relationship; for two subjects to effectively talk to each other, an affective circulation should have already been established between them, helping the child to advance from the position of dependence and passivity ("passive object-love") to the intersubjective relationship with the objects of his choice. Trauma, understood as a fracture in the child's omnipotent gesture, therefore implies a disavowal of the infantile language of tenderness and the *truth* it carries.

3.6 Splitting: identification with the aggressor and traumatic progression

In 1923, Ferenczi dedicates a few lines to the dream of the "clever baby", reported by several analysands, "[...] in which the newly born, quite young children, or babies in the cradle, appear, who are able to talk or write fluently, [...] carry on intelligent conversations, deliver harangues, give learned explanations, and so on" (Ferenczi, 1923/1994g, p. 349). The same archetypal figure of the wise baby appears in fairy tales, myths, and religious traditions.[8] At the time, Ferenczi believed that this dream would symbolize the desire for a "reversal of the contrary situation of the child" (Ferenczi, 1923/1994g, p. 349), that is, dependent on the care — wisdom and knowledge — of adults.

In the early 1930s, in the context of the development of his trauma theory, the dream is once again taken up along with other dreams and autosymbolic materials as a representation of the "*narcissistic split of the self*" to which the subject resorts in the face of traumatic disavowal. As such, Ferenczi (1931/1994o, p. 135) reports dreams of patients in which the head, separated from the body, walks on its own feet or is connected to the trunk by a thin thread;[9] or even fantasies in which a predator attacks a jellyfish with claws and teeth, and the jellyfish dodges the blows and returns to its spherical shape afterwards. The assumption is that these psychical materials express the subject's "passive resistance" to environmental aggressions, as well as the splitting of their personality "into a suffering, brutally destroyed part and a part which, as it were, knows everything but feels nothing" (Ferenczi, 1931/1994o, p. 135).

The traumatic situation urges the abandoned subject to create, through splitting, a self-perceptive instance for himself to replace his absent caregivers. "Part of the person adopts the role of father or mother in relation to the rest, thereby undoing, as it were, the fact of being left deserted" (Ferenczi, 1931/1994o, p. 135). Ferenczi thus emphasizes the tendency of morally and physically traumatized children to show signs of early maturity and wisdom. They become people who tend to motherly surround others and help them by passing on the knowledge acquired through their own suffering. They are the "family psychiatrists"

8 I refer the reader to the scene of Siddhartha's birth in the film *The Little Buddha*, by Bernardo Bertolucci (1993).

9 Winnicott (1945/2000a) describes psychotic experiences of depersonalization very similar to the dreams described by Ferenczi's analysands.

(and future candidates for care practices, including psychoanalysts).[10] In this sense, by providing the autosymbolic clues for a comprehension of the narcissistic splitting, the dream of the wise baby acquires a new understanding. It is no longer an expression of the modest desire for independence from adults, but the effective need to mature early in order to survive, establishing a pathological "traumatic progression" (Ferenczi, 1933/1994q, p. 165).

Concerning sexual traumas and those resulting from corporal punishment, splitting would appear as the child's response when incapable of defensive alloplastic reactions in the face of fear of maddened adults. The child would then resort to autoplastic reactions through which he identifies himself with the aggressor by using a kind of mimicry, guessing the aggressor's desires and automatically obeying their wishes (Ferenczi, 1933/1994q, p. 162). Identification with the aggressor is an operation in which the external threat becomes intrapsychic, which would allow the child to (imaginarily) regain control over the intolerable situation, and even revert to the previous situation of tenderness, deauthorizing any perceptions related to the aggression suffered. By somewhat numbing the traumatic anguish, the split subject takes refuge in the position of an "observer", oblivious to the events of the world and his suffering (*cf.* Verztman, 2002).

However, the burden of identifying with the aggressor is, on the one hand, a loss of "confidence in the testimony of his own senses" after deauthorizing the perception of the traumatic event (Ferenczi, 1933/1994q, p. 162); on the other hand, since the prevailing version is the one brought about through disavowal, the subject ends up incorporating the feeling of guilt typically seen in the adult aggressor.

A frequent effect of identification with the aggressor is the sudden emergence, in the child, of faculties found in the adults he mirrors. Ferenczi (1933/1994q, p. 165) employs a striking metaphor

---

10 As analysands, they tend to "take care" of their analysts, avoiding criticism and the expression of any hostility whatsoever, which, at the limit, hinders the analysis.

for this process, described as pathological prematurity or traumatic progression. "It is natural to compare this with the precocious maturity of the fruit that was injured by a bird or insect" (Ferenczi, 1933/1994q, p. 165). The image fairly illustrates the notion of a split between an omniscient, but numb, intelligible part; and another part, the sensitive core of the subject carrying the feeling of self, destroyed.[11] Seeking an approximation with Freud's metapsychology (from which he never wished to depart), Ferenczi demonstrates that the split subjectivity would configure the "assumption of a mind which consists only of the id and super-ego" (Ferenczi, 1933/1994q, p. 163), which, having significantly compromised egoic functions of mediation, would be unable to assert itself in situations of anguish provoked by helplessness, i.e., situations that require the psychic apparatus to use its competences of mourning and consequent re-signification of the self and the objects.

The subjectivities which are thus described, because they "identify themselves with the aggressor" (Ferenczi, 1933/1994q, p. 162), fail to find ways to escape from the adherence to the object which, preserved from the work of detachment promoted by the exercise of affective ambivalence, remains ingrained as an ideal in the psyche. Their dependence and subservience to the object incorporated as a tyrannical superego are therefore perpetuated, resembling the description of masochism, a psychopathological instance that was the focus of Freud's attention in the last years of his work (*cf.* Freud, 1924/1980l; 1928[1927]/1980o; 1930[1929]1980p).[12]

A third and final modality of trauma is described by Ferenczi as the "terrorism of suffering", which is more harmful than any form of explicit

---

11 It is not difficult to recognize the influence of the notion of narcissistic splitting on Winnicott's conceptions of the true and false self, resulting from the basic split of personality (Winnicott, 1960).

12 I refer the reader to the instigating essay by Herbert Marcuse (1998), in which the philosopher, without citing Ferenczi, develops formulations about a subject consisting solely of the *id* and superego through static identifications found in the "fatherless society".

violence suffered by the subject. In this case, Ferenczi describes the effects of maternal depression — "a mother complaining of her constant miseries" — on the small child, who thus finds himself transformed into a "real mother substitute" who is in charge of taking care of his own mother. The relationship of care is then reversed, and precociously mature children, in an attempt to recover the primary tenderness, are forced "to put to rights all disorder in the family, to burden, so to speak, their own tender shoulders with the load of all the others" (Ferenczi, 1933/1994q, p. 166).

It is significant to compare Freud's use of the figure of the child as a representative of the repressed with the images of the wise baby and the traumatized child presented by Ferenczi. The Freudian child is the malicious child who denounces social hypocrisy by making unexpected comments — as in Andersen's parable *The Emperor's New Clothes (1837)*, in which the child is the one who reveals that the emperor is naked. The Freudian child then holds a knowledge that, with the incidence of repression, became unavailable to the adult. It is the infantile — in the form of fantasies, anxieties, and sexual theories — that emerges, in a startling manner, in the accounts of Freud's neurotic patients. In the Wolf Man case study, Freud (1918[1914]/1955b, p. 103) writes: "For my own observations show that we have rated the powers of children too low and that there is no knowing what they cannot be given credit for".

On the other hand, the split child (and the child who survives in the traumatized adult), precociously matured, is the one who can no longer find a pathway towards his sensitive core — home to his creative power — and has unlearned how to play games. His knowledge is bland, built from an incorporation of the aggressor, synonymous with loss of authenticity. In these cases, the tripod that constitutes the Freudian method — free association, principle of abstinence, and interpretation of the resistances and the repressed — proves to be inoperative, since the emergence of unconscious formations ceases to manifest itself as an effect of the circulation of words. Consequently, the psychoanalyst's challenge becomes that of opposing traumatic progression, with the possibility for the analysand to regress to the playfulness of tenderness within the transference situation.

In fact, the clinical style developed by Ferenczi with difficult patients led him to "temper materially the antithesis, hitherto so sharp, between the analysis of children and that of adults", giving rise to "play-analysis" even in the clinical practice with adults (Ferenczi, 1931/19940, p. 127–131). In this way, both the repetitions of traumatic experiences and the tender and playful manifestations became a part of the psychoanalytic setting (once again, since the scenario resembled that of the treatment of hysterics in the 19th century). "Not infrequently patients [...] produce little stories which they have made up, or even poems and rhymes", Ferenczi writes, adding that "[...] sometimes they ask for a pencil so as to make us a present of a drawing, generally of a very naive sort" (Ferenczi, 1931/19940, p. 133).

This demonstrates that clinical psychoanalytic treatment of difficult patients — meaning those who, due to their defenses in the face of traumatic disavowal fail to adapt to the traditional technique — has elected as its privileged object the expression of the patients' split sensitive components. This is certainly a laborious task, but not impossible, for as long as any vital élan remains present.

It is interesting to note that Ferenczi, theorist of the wise baby and the traumatized, precociously matured child, has been nicknamed "the *enfant terrible*" of psychoanalysis.

3.7 *"Releasing the patient's tongue": trauma and testimony in clinical practice*

Ferenczi's return to the problem of trauma from the mid-1920s was motivated not only by the impasses of the clinic, which led him to diagnose a severe impairment in the identification processes of "difficult patients", but also by his experience on the front in World War I, as a physician in the Hungarian army. As Gustavo Dean-Gomes (2019) underlines, coming into contact with the traumatic neuroses experienced by soldiers sparked the interest of several analysts, so much so that an entire symposium was dedicated to war neuroses during the International Budapest Congress of 1918. In hindsight, one can imagine that Ferenczi's heightened sensitivity to trauma originating from social and political phenomena like war contributed to the decisive new direction he was able to indicate in the understanding of the importance of otherness in the production of disruptive experiences.

After the abandonment of seduction theory, which had proposed that sexual abuse of a child by an adult was the source of trauma, the role of the other in producing a traumatic phenomenon was, if not entirely ignored, greatly underestimated by the psychoanalytic community. When returning to the issue of trauma in *Beyond the Pleasure Principle*, Freud (1920/1980j) emphasized that the source of trauma lies in the excess of excitement promoted by the work of the death instinct in the psyche, without privileging the role of otherness in its production. The Freudian trauma continues to be a *sexual trauma* — because it refers to a defusion of instincts — even if the influence of Thanatos in its constitution is still considered.

On the other hand, in Ferenczi's description, the traumatic event is consummated only at the time of disavowal perpetrated by the other, whom the traumatized subject trusted and from whom he sought assistance to represent the violence suffered. Thus, by proposing a *relational* reading of the Freudian concept of *Verleugnung* — the denial of castration that is found in perversions — Ferenczi lays the foundation for the conception of *social trauma*, demonstrating that the non-recognition of a vulnerable subject's narrative of suffering corresponds to the disavowal of his experience and testimony by the other to whom he turned in the social and political sphere.

As such, if the Freudian *sexual trauma*, even when originating from an external intrusion, characterizes an intrapsychic operation, the notion of *social trauma* exposes a fracture in the operation of recognition in the sphere of social and political relations (*cf.* Gondar, 2012). Faced with the threat of death, exclusion, segregation, and violence, we are all children in search of a testimony that can help us recover our dignity after being affected by the indifference of those to whom we turned for help.

Inspired by the relational and social conception of Ferenczi's traumatogenesis, I identify some useful tools for reflection on the clinical dimension of testimony, and its acceptance by the other, whether in cultural life or in the course of an analytical treatment. What follows, based on the iconographic and written production of an Auschwitz survivor, is an example of how disavowal impacts victims of social violence, and also how psychoanalysis, by offering the possibility of a testimony for the experience of indifference, can aid in producing meaning from the traumatic experience. This will allow us to conclude that working through trauma requires us to invent an individual language that can create a unique style for saying that which cannot be said.

3.7.1 The aesthetics of disavowal: Maryan's *Notebooks*

We were introduced to Maryan S. Maryan by Alan Osmo (2016), who, during his research on the links between trauma and testimony, found the artist's *Notebooks*.

Maryan S. Maryan was the artistic name adopted by Pinchas Burstein, born in Poland in 1927, who was sent to Auschwitz and other camps in his early teens for being Jewish and survived the concentration experience with severe physical and psychological after-effects. After the war, he went to a refugee camp in Germany, emigrating in 1947 to

Israel, where he began his artistic studies. He moved to Paris in 1950, where he completed his training at the *École Nationale des Beaux Arts*, becoming a well-known representative of expressionism, and being awarded, in 1976, the honorary title of *Chevalier de l'Ordre des Arts et des Lettres* from France. In 1962, Maryan moved to New York, where he remained until his death in 1977, at the age of fifty. During his career, his work was exhibited in many European countries, in the United States, Israel, and Venezuela, gaining prominence in important galleries and museums.

Looking for help for his suffering, which had worsened over the years, he underwent analysis between 1971 and 1972. Because he was unable to speak — about the relatives who died in Auschwitz, his time in the camps, or even his childhood — his psychoanalyst suggested that he draw and, through the drawings, recover his memory and his history.[13] Maryan filled a total of nine notebooks with 478 drawings in crayon on paper, with motifs ranging from his childhood in Poland to his own analytical experience, going through the nightmare of the concentration camps. The *Notebooks* became public in their entirety only in 2013, in an exhibition held at the *Musée d'Art et d'Histoire du Judaïsme*, in Paris (Maryan, 2013), and today they belong to the collection of the *Centre Georges Pompidou*.[14]

Maryan was the only member of his family to survive the Nazi regime. During his imprisonment in the camps he survived a firing squad, by which he was shot twice (once in the face and once in the neck), and on another occasion, close to his release, he was wounded and ended up having one of his legs amputated. These events are present in many of the images drawn by Maryan in his *Notebooks*.

13 For the controversy regarding what actually led Maryan to conceive his *Notebooks*, I refer the reader to Alan Osmo (2018).

14 See https://www.centrepompidou.fr/fr/recherche/oeuvres?terms=maryan%20carnet

I chose to discuss Maryan's case in this chapter about trauma in Ferenczi's work based on a number of factors. First, according to the version published in the catalog of the Paris exhibition, this material is clinical material, i.e., drawings produced in the course of an analytical process as a means of seeking to express, aided by the transference field, the impact of traumatic events previously experienced. Furthermore, because Maryan was a victim of social and political violence, the testimony contained in his *Notebooks* refers to experiences shared by millions of people — incarceration in concentration camps — and, in this sense, has the potential to evoke a collective human trauma, as was the case with Primo Levi's writing (*cf.* Osmo & Kupermann, 2017; *cf.* Soreanu, 2018). According to this hypothesis, his drawings would have the ability to express the transindividual affect of the horror shared not only by those who died or by those who survived the camps, and their direct descendants but also by all those who are outraged by this bleak chapter of our recent history.

It is known that victims of psychic trauma often do not find resources for the representation of what they have experienced, thus using the modality of "showing" something related to the experience in the presence of someone significant as an attempt to achieve witness, through *figurability* (*Darstellung*),[15] of the pain evoked by unrepresentable memory (*cf.* Bastos, 2018). Maryan's drawings provide viewers with the imagery required to evoke the unspeakable, favoring the search for the production of meaning for the indelible events produced by the *Shoah* in those who are willing to get in touch with the expression of their agony. His *Notebooks* thus shamelessly illustrate the contemporary face of Medusa: *indifference to the suffering of the other through the disavowal of his testimony.*

15 On the psychoanalytic concept of figurability, see Freud (1900/1980d; 1900/1980e) and Botella and Botella (2002).

Due to limited space, I will reproduce here only five drawings through which the reader will be able to recognize the most fundamental elements of Ferenczi's theory of trauma. In all of them, there is an evident unrealism; his *Notebooks* do not intend to be an objective representation of what was experienced by Maryan in the camps but to witness the horror imprinted by the traumatic events on his subjectivity and, at the same time, reach the viewer's sensitivity. One can thus understand Maryan's option for the grotesque style which, in addition to having the potential to convey the intensity of his affectation, seems to indicate the very movement of *regression* provided by the analytical space. There is, in fact, something dreamlike, and even hallucinatory, in his drawings, which tends to refer his viewer to the terrifying universe of childhood nightmares, as well as the leaking body full of holes that defecates, vomits, and cries, source of the infantile erogenous omnipotence (see Chapter 4) that we insist on repressing (Figure 1).

Figure 1 Notebook 4.

Source: https://www.centrepompidou.fr/fr/recherche/oeuvres?terms=maryan%20carnet.

In addition, the symbols representing Judaism (the Star of David) and Nazism (the swastika) are frequently seen simultaneously present in the same character, revealing the *identification with the aggressor* produced by the traumatic event (Figure 2).

Figure 2 Notebook 4.

Source: https://www.centrepompidou.fr/fr/recherche/oeuvres?terms=maryan%20carnet.

The witness who laughs at his own suffering, often in the form of a skull, promptly reminds us of the traumatic disavowal (Figures 3 and 4). Lastly, the reader will be able to see that the character who disavows is often situated behind the one who suffers, who is lying in front of him, alluding to the analytic setting itself; this way, the psychoanalyst appears in the *Notebooks* both as a witness capable of recognizing the trauma victim's agony and as the potential *aggressor* who disavows it (Figures 3 and 4).

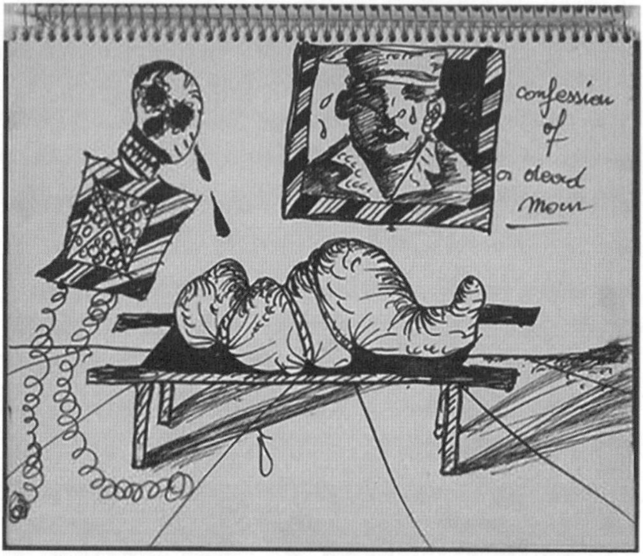

Figure 3 Notebook 6.

Source: https://www.centrepompidou.fr/fr/recherche/oeuvres?terms=maryan%20carnet.

Figure 4 Notebook 9.

Source: https://www.centrepompidou.fr/fr/recherche/oeuvres?terms=maryan%20carnet.

In fact, in Figure 5, the character who is crying desperately addresses a skull — the same one that appears in Figure 3, representing the analyst who carries an object that resembles a mirror — exclaiming: "You dirty shrink".

Figure 5 Notebook 6.

Source: https://www.centrepompidou.fr/fr/recherche/oeuvres?terms=maryan%20carnet.

Only one psychoanalyst, Gérard Wajcman (2013), contributed an essay to Maryan's *Notebooks* exhibition catalog. The curious thing about his writing is that, despite making excellent comments on the expressive power of drawings, he criticizes Maryan's psychoanalyst for having encouraged him to draw and therefore not allowing space for spoken language during the artist's treatment. For Wajcman, the drawings give us a silencing effect precisely because of the paradoxical fact of having the competence to express so intensely the traumatic dimension of the artist's experience.

The immediate approximation that can be made with the presence of drawings in the analytical setting is with child psychoanalysis. Also according to Wajcman, in child analyses the drawings would serve to open up the field for words, not carrying any working-through value. We are aware of the controversies in this sense when it comes to notions of playing in the clinic with children. Winnicott (1975/2000d), for example, in a well-known passage from *Playing and Reality*, differentiating noun from verb, warned us that psychoanalysts, ever since Klein, would have paid too much attention to the content of games, underestimating the role of playing in the clinic. Before him, however, in "Child-Analysis in the Analysis of Adults", Ferenczi (1931/1994o) had observed how the regression favored by the flexibility of the analytic setting would provide, even to the adult, resources for "analysis through playing", showing the way, through playful and truly infantile manifestations, for symbolizing and working through traumatic scars. Recalling this comment, some analysands even asked for a pencil to sketch generally very *primitive* drawings. Ferenczi is categorical concerning the richness of these rudimentary — because they are infantile — productions over the course of an analysis:

> *What is important is that one should not abuse this phase, in which the subject is unquestionably much more helpless than usual by urging upon his unresisting mind one's own theories and fantasies. On the contrary, we ought to use our undeniably great influence here to deepen the patient's* capacity for producing *his own material (Ferenczi, 1931/1994o, p. 134)*

Thus, for Ferenczi, regression and playfulness are integral parts of the setting in the clinic of trauma, with no effective separation between form and content in listening to the emergence of unconscious material, referring us to the appreciation of expressiveness and of the aesthetic aspect of the clinic (a problem I will develop in the next chapter). Ferenczi (Ferenczi, 1931/1994o, p. 134) even creates a neologism, proposing that instead of attempting to "suggest [...] things *into* the patient", the analysis should create the conditions for the analysand to be able to suggest his memories, phantoms, agonies, and desires "*out*", which would be clinically much more useful.

We also observe that in many of Maryan's drawings, we have the co-presence of words or even entire sentences and images, in the style of journalistic cartoons. Furthermore, as we have no news of the use of his drawings in the analytic setting — i.e., whether or not they gave access to words in his analysis — we cannot agree or disagree with Wajcman's criticism. In any case, based on the above, one must ask whether the act of *testimony* present in the composition of his drawings would not, in itself, give rise to analytical effects. If so, drawing and captioning would be equivalent to speaking… in the language of tenderness that was possible for Maryan.

***

The second key element evoked by his drawings is the relationship between the wars that decisively marked the 20th century and the reflection on trauma promoted by psychoanalysis. Wajcman (*2013*) refers to Walter Benjamin, whose observation of the end of the possibility of narrative[16] is due to his perception that the combatants returned *mute* from the trenches of World War I; not richer by experience, but without words that could communicate any lived experience. The French used the expression "*gueules cassées*" ("broken faces"), created by Colonel Picot, to refer to the way that the restraints of war trauma affected combatants' possibilities of expression.

We know how much World War I and the care offered to victims of "war neuroses" (Ferenczi, 1916/1992b; Freud, 1919/1980i) were responsible for Freud and Ferenczi's diving back into the issue of trauma. In this sense, despite acknowledging the elements of trauma that cannot be represented, in the face of the mutism that fell on the 20th century, psychoanalysis has nevertheless made a clinical-political

16 On the end of the narrative, see Benjamin (1986).

decision: to persevere in the work of *saying* what cannot be said, *symbolizing* the unnameable, *testifying* to the muted, and *expressing* the intangible, which requires a particular ethic and aesthetic.

Still insisting on the fact that listening to trauma necessarily evokes the political dimension of psychoanalysis, I understand that the theorization of social trauma based on the concept of *disavowal* points to the dimension of struggle to which Freud refers in several moments of his work: the conflict between the psychical instances, resignifying it as a *struggle for recognition*, in the sense of the approximation between the Hegelian notion of recognition and the operation provided by the clinical psychology proposed by Jessica Benjamin (1988).[17] In her analysis, "recognition is the response from the other that gives meaning to feelings, intentions, and actions of the self. It allows the self to be tangibly aware of its agency and authorship" (p. 12).

In clinical psychoanalysis, the need for reparation of the traumatic disavowal summons the sensitive presence of the psychoanalyst; according to the argument developed throughout this chapter, the analyst plays the role of a witness to the analysand's gesture, aiming to provide recognition of his hitherto unnameable pain (*cf.* Gondar & Antonello, 2016). The formulation that it is mostly on the failure of the *time of testimony* that the psychoanalyst works in the clinical treatment of traumatized subjectivities forms the foundation of the irreplaceable task of recognition in psychoanalytic practice.

***

The last point that I would like to highlight in Maryan's drawings is the omnipresence of the grotesque style, in which dream and hallucinatory unrealism predominate: a bridge between the infantile and the monstrous, and the presence of the incontinent body; a body

17 See also *Struggle for Recognition: The Moral Grammar of Social Conflicts*, by Axel Honneth (2009).

of orifices (also caused by bullet holes) through which secretions and excrement — tears, vomit, blood, and feces — are shamelessly displayed.

I said previously that the work of saying what cannot be said requires a particular ethics and aesthetic. In fact, if we consider the process of production of meaning based on Freud's comments (1905/1980g) in *Jokes and their Relation to the Unconscious*, in which the *Witz* produces unconscious effects *only* insofar as it affects the "third person" (its audience), we conceive that there is a certain manner or style of speaking that allows for the revelation of the repressed, which has the effect of promoting the social bond, in the place of constraint or aggression towards the other. This is because to Freud the same element that produces horror or estrangement (*das unheimliche*) can produce shared laughter (*cf.* Kupermann, 2003, Chapter 6). Some viewers find a subtle humorous effect in Maryan's drawings that does not seem to contradict their terrifying effect. In this case, one can see humor and horror assuming symmetrical functions, though at opposite extremes, exposing the ambivalence between the terrifying and the grotesque — a quality, according to Vernant (1991), of the "monstrous".

Vernant's deeper reading of the "monstrous" in ancient Greece, to which *Witz* is affiliated, allows us to get closer to the problem. In Greek mythology, there is a kinship between two prominent figures that evoke representations of otherness: the gorgon Medusa and Baubó, one of the Graeae, who amuses Demeter with her antics. The common trait to both is the grimace, both the one that terrifies us — as in the portrait of Medusa by Caravaggio — and the sexual masks of Baubó that make Demeter laugh.

Also according to Vernant, the grimace, through the disfigurement of the features that make up the human figure, expresses

> *an effect of* disconcerting strangeness *that expresses a form of the monstrous that oscillates between two extremes: the*

> *horror of the terrifying and the hilarity of the grotesque [...] the monstrous face whose equivalent it is in certain respects, also has the power to provoke both sacred fear and liberating laughter (Vernant, 1991, p. 113)*

Maryan's drawings, with their blend of the infantile and the terrifying, with their incontinent bodies and the omnipresence of death in the form of a sarcastic grimace/swastika, seem to reveal the attempt to find a language capable of giving contour to the obscenities that the tragedy-history of the concentration camps had revealed. In fact, behind the appearance of a civilizing order promoted by instrumental reason, there was the absurdity through which human dignity was reduced to bare life, as demonstrated by Agamben (2002). In Maryan, the expression of this type of horror, veiled by the efficiency of the death industry, summons the grotesque style, in which the monstrous is aligned with sarcasm and ridicule, exerting a hypnotic effect on us capable of provoking an eloquent silence.

In psychoanalysis, an authentic trauma work is that which can create a possible language for the expression of a hitherto unspeakable experience, a supreme paradox that continues to provoke the desire and imagination of analysts. Nevertheless, we know that: what cannot be said, can be shown. But that which can be shown gains meaning only in the face of the testimony of *another* who opposes the prevailing indifference of our cultural life.

4. The turning point of 1928 and the principles for an ethics of care in psychoanalysis

Here again an important source of masochism:
pain as the alleviation of other, greater pains.
(Ferenczi, 1932/1988, p. 23)

The ideas developed in this chapter aim to shed light on the principles that govern the clinical style established, as from what I call the *turning point of 1928,* in the psychoanalytic field by Sándor Ferenczi. Not by chance, the choice of the term "turning point" aims to show that there is a relationship between the *Ferenczian turning point* of 1928 and the more widely known *Freudian turning point* of 1920, characterized by the formulation of the death instinct and the second topic of the psychic apparatus.[1]

In fact, as demonstrated by Balint (2014), Ferenczi's clinical originality could already be found in *Thalassa*, published in 1924, but

1 In a personal communication, Renato Mezan declared that he believed that the term "turning point", well-known in Brazilian psychoanalytic literature, in reference to the theoretical change made by Freud from 1920 onwards, was originally due to Laplanche and, therefore, a translation of the French expression *tournant*. However, this reference has not yet been found.

would have gained momentum in 1928, with the presentation of essays on the elasticity of the technique and on the issue of termination of analysis. Partially following Balint, I believe it is possible to say that the inventiveness of Ferenczi's clinical thought resides in the intrinsic and necessary development of the 1928 trilogy, which constitutes a true founding milestone in the history of psychoanalytic ideas.

Thalassa introduces readers to the Lamarckist postulates of "bioanalysis", which had been in development for almost a decade by Ferenczi, and also by Freud[2] — with emphasis on the structuring dimension of the catastrophes suffered by species throughout the adaptation process that led to the emergence of *Homo sapiens*, as well as the healing powers of regression, which motivates the behavior of sexual beings. Yet, the essay does not sufficiently explore the unfolding of such theses in clinical theory and in ideas about the transference encounter — these are in the trilogy that comprises the turning point of 1928.

However, what would determine a *turning point* in the field of psychoanalysis? Every psychoanalyst we effectively consider to be an author developed his contributions to Freud in at least three aspects: first, by creating their own metapsychological categories, in reference to the process of subjective constitution and the psychopathology that corresponds to it; secondly, by establishing a clinical theory capable of dealing with the psychopathological conditions described, according to his conceptions about the origins of human suffering; and lastly, by proposing ethical-political-institutional reflections that refer both to the direction of the treatment — or its conception of cure — and to criticism about the psychoanalyst's own resistance to the power of affectation of the clinical encounter, and the competences that are required for him to properly perform his craft. This is what can be found, notwithstanding evident differences, in Klein, Winnicott, and Lacan, among others.

2 See *Transference Neuroses: A Synthesis* (Freud, 1915/1987).

Thus, it can be considered that the *turning point* occurs when these three dimensions of the work of a psychoanalyst effectively indicate a change of direction in the paths (*wege*) of the theoretical-clinical thinking of psychoanalysis. A turning point would thus differ from the conception of a "return to Freud's truth" emphasized by Lacan (1956/1998), coming closer to the exercise of the "author function" present and active in the production and transmission of knowledge concerning the field of discursivity, in which psychoanalysis participates — described by Michael Foucault (1969/2000). The "author function" is exercised by returning to the work of the initiator (Freud, in the case of psychoanalysis) due to a certain type of "oblivion" which, far from being an *accident en route*, seems to be inherent to the very constitution of discursivity.

The "return to origin" provoked by the *turning point* would, for this reason, refer less to the ultimate truth that would risk restricting the power of the act of creation of a discursivity, and more to an opening, through the acknowledgement of differences, to the richness of the inaugural work, obscured by the pseudo-completeness of current readings.

4.1 The turning point of 1928

In 1928, Sándor Ferenczi presented three essays to the psychoanalytic community, each dedicated to one of the aspects of developing an authorial work in psychoanalysis: metapsychology/psychopathology, clinical or technical theory, and ethical-political-institutional considerations. The first is "The Adaptation of the Family to the Child" (1928/1994k), in which Ferenczi twists the concept of adaptation used by Freud, and to some extent emphasized by Ferenczi himself in his provocative 1913 essay "Stages in the Development of the Sense of Reality" (1913/1994d), according to which the instinctual child, moved by the pleasure principle, should adapt "unilaterally" to the reality principle imposed by the world of objects through successive structuring traumas.[3] After the publication of this essay, enriched by the subsequent developments by Balint and Winnicott, the prevailing notion for psychoanalysts identified with object relations thinking would be that the primary adaptation — a condition for the subject's experience of creative omnipotence — is the one promoted by the environment upon the arrival of the *infans (cf.* Gurfinkel, 2017).

The second essay, "The Elasticity of Psychoanalytical Technique" (1928/1994l), should be read as an extension of the first, since in it Ferenczi extracts the clinical consequences of his environmentalist perspective. His argument could be summarized by the idea that it is not the analysand who should take on the task of adapting to the psychoanalytic technique (at that time defined by free association, the principle of abstinence in transference, and interpretation). It is the analyst who needs to show the required flexibility to treat individuals who, until then, were considered impossible to analyze.

Note that in the same gesture promoted by "The Elasticity of the Psychoanalytical Technique", psychoanalysis itself opened up to the so-called "difficult patients" (the name first given to what are now known in Anglo-Saxon literature as borderline cases), limit-cases (in French literature), or narcissistic pathologies. Ferenczi effectively believed these were traumatized patients. It is also in this essay that Ferenczi, provoked by the challenge manifested by analysands who had been unsuccessful in the connection processes that constitute primary narcissism and ego integration, proposes the term *empathy* to name expanded modalities of clinical interaction. The difficulties presented by traumatized subjects in complying with the rule of free association, dreaming, committing slips of the tongue, and including the analyst in the field of updating unconscious infantile *imagos*, as

3 We will show, later in the book, that the same essay includes an active dimension of the Ferenczian child, in which the child gains his/her sense of reality through a movement propelled by the driving force of his/her primordial omnipotence. See also Kupermann (2003, Chapter 2).

advocated by the then-current conception of transference, demanded from the psychoanalyst a *sensitive presence* if some possibility of clinical intervention was to be preserved (*cf.* Kupermann, 2008). Empathy (*Einfühlung*), literally "feeling within", indicates a requirement for the analyst to feel the other within himself, which paved the way for the reflections that flourished in the English school from the 1950s onwards regarding countertransference.

Lastly, in "The Problem of Termination of the Analysis" (1927/1994j), the essay that closes the trilogy, Ferenczi takes the logically necessary step: the style of clinical psychoanalysis inspired by his environmentalist perspective — for schematic purposes I will name the clinical style he created the *empathic style* — demanded from the psychoanalyst a sensitive and affective availability differentiated from that proposed by the classical Freudian method, which we could also designate, schematically, as an *interpretive style*. Thus, reflection on training analyses and their effects on the metapsychology of analysts would be a *sine qua non* for the success of the psychoanalytic experience. It is important, however, to emphasize that one style is not opposed to the other. Freud certainly did not fail to conceive the importance of empathy, just as Ferenczi did not abandon the interpretive instrument. It is, therefore, a question more of emphasis than difference. But, as I intend to demonstrate, in some clinical situations the emphasis does itself make a considerable difference.

Indeed, the tone of "The Problem of Termination of the Analysis" is extremely critical of the training of analysts, pointing in an important ethical direction by formulating that at the horizon of the end of treatment would be the deconstruction of narcissism (pathological, as we will see) and of the superego — indeed, in the analysis of analysts, the undoing of what Balint (1948; 1954) called the "*technical superego*", referring to the rigid adherence of psychoanalysts to theoretical systems of affiliation that prevents them from analyzing by using the free play of faculties necessary to expand their imaginative capacity.

Having thus introduced the trilogy that comprises the turning point in psychoanalysis provoked by Sándor Ferenczi in 1928, I will now look, first, at "The Adaptation of the Family to the Child", demonstrating how this essay intends to confront Freud's second theory of anxiety.

4.2 From pain to the joy of existence

In "Inhibitions, Symptoms and Anxiety", Freud (1926/1980m) presents two important pillars of his last theory, referring to the death instinct and the second topic of the psychic apparatus. The argument — actually a debate — revolves around the publication of Otto Rank's book, *The Trauma of Birth* (which was dedicated to Freud), in which an unprecedented clinical optimism can be found in the last chapter, supported by the idea that the management of transference could promote a "second" birth, due to the separation of the analyst, as foreseen by the liquidation of transference, that would now be no longer traumatic (Rank, 1924/1929). Freud criticizes both Rank's metapsychology and his clinical model.

Firstly, Freud (1926/1980m) believes birth would simply be the prototype of later separations, such as weaning, the acquisition of physiological control involved in cleanliness, entering school life, amorous connections, entering the workforce, all of which accompany the process of subjective maturation and socialization. In other words, the acquisition of a sense of reality would necessarily be traumatic, since the human being is born in a state of helplessness and dependence (due to his biological immaturity) and any threat of abandonment or fear of losing the love of the mother or caregiver sends him back to helplessness, the primary source of all anxiety. According to this conception, in adult life, anxiety is no longer directly related to the other on whom the child depended but is activated by the action of the superego, the Other incorporated into the psyche.

Furthermore, Freud makes a severe criticism of a clinical model that intended to cure the trauma of birth, indicating that traumatic experiences are constitutive of the psychic apparatus and hence inexorable. With his characteristic irony, Freud uses an accurate analogy: you cannot put out a house fire by removing the overturned kerosene lamp that caused it. The Freudian lamp is nothing less than the drive, with emphasis on the death instinct (the incurable incendiary). Thus, every threat of loss of the object, or actual loss — in other words, every drive defusion — is potentially destructive, requiring an onerous work of bonding on the part of the psychic apparatus.

In this sense, Freud moves away from the privilege attributed by Rank to therapeutic regression, and the notion of a *new birth* provided by the transference experience,[4] reaffirming the primacy of his intrapsychic model, anchored in the drive paradigm and in the irreparable conflict between the instances, which characterizes the field of neuroses.

Ferenczi, Rank's former partner in the publication of "The Further Development of an Active Therapy in Psycho-Analysis" (*cf.* Ferenczi, 1920/1994f), enters the debate criticizing both Rank and Freud. His argument is based on what can be called (after the publication of "The Adaptation of the Family to the Child") *psychoanalytic environmentalism*, illustrated by two formulations supported by the following tenets:

1. "[…] birth is a sort of triumph for the child and must surely exert as such an influence on its whole life" (Ferenczi, 1928/1994k, p. 64), and therefore is not a trauma;
2. The state of helplessness and consequent dependence of the child on the adult implies that the *relationship between the adults and the*

4 This brings us to the idea of a *new beginning* formulated by Balint (1932/1994) and popularized in the English school by Winnicott (1954/2000c).

child can be effectively traumatic. In this way, the state of helplessness is not the source of trauma *per se*, but only within the relationship with the other.[5] Just as there is no baby without a caregiver, there is also no helplessness without a relational perspective that involves the presence of the other (the same theoretical treatment is given by Ferenczi to the death instinct, which he describes as a founding myth evoked by Freud, in the sense that both Eros and Thanatos depend on the relationship established with/by the other caregiver, as I will demonstrate later).

The joyful statement that birth is a triumph presupposes, on the one hand, that the fetus is biologically ready to be born, i.e., that the digestive and respiratory systems are already mature enough to come into contact with the environment outside of the mother's womb; on the other hand, the family, representing the environment *adapted* to the baby's bio-psycho-physiological needs, makes the transition from the mother's uterus to her arms, and from there to the world, as smooth as possible. One can easily recognize in this notion the ideas of Winnicott (*cf.* 1952/2000b) regarding the *good enough mother*, the mother sufficiently well-adapted to the neonate. Further, the formulation of a triumph of birth also contradicts the figure of the "melancholic baby" presented by Ferenczi himself in his 1913 essay, "Stages in the Development of the Sense of Reality", which persisted in psychoanalytic thinking. On this aspect, it is worth noting the clearly provocative epigraph chosen by Rank for *The Trauma of Birth*: the words from Silenus to Midas evoked by Nietzsche in *The Birth of Tragedy, or: Hellenism and Pessimism* (one can see that Rank's book title is inspired by Nietzsche's, inverting it and adapting it to psychoanalytic terminology: The tragedy [trauma] of birth). Silenus says, "The very best is quite unattainable for you: it

5 I remind the reader of the provocative article by Jurandir Freire Costa (2000) entitled "*O Mito Psicanalítico do Desamparo*" ("The Psychoanalytic Myth of Helplessness", in English).

is, not to be born, not to exist, to be Nothing. But the next best for you is — to die soon" (Nietzsche *apud* Rank, 1924/1929, p. V).[6]

If it were possible to choose, the fetus (certainly melancholic) would prefer not to be born… to preserve his omnipotence in the mother's womb. From 1928 onwards, however, out of vital exuberance and with the proof of joy, the fetus wants to be born… and is so.

4.3 *Omnipotence and traumatogenesis*

We thus arrive at a decisive problem in the recovery of traumatogenesis: that of *omnipotence* and its relationship with psychopathological etiology. Psychoanalyst Jay Frankel (2017) is precise in indicating the articulation made by Ferenczi between the emergence of pathological narcissism and the traumatic event, analyzing the main effects of the latter on subjectivity: traumatic progression through identification with the aggressor, and the omnipotence fantasies arising from it.

As seen in the previous chapter, Ferenczi (1931/19940) posits that in the traumatic situation, the aggressor is a loved one from whom the child cannot detach himself, at the risk of falling into abandonment. As a defensive device, the child identifies with the *aggressor object*, promoting a narcissistic splitting into a part that "knows everything but feels nothing" (the omnipotent part of the traumatic progression) and another sensitive, destroyed part (Ferenczi, 1931/19940, p. 135). The metaphor proposed by Ferenczi (1933/1994q) of the worm-eaten fruit — ripe on the outside, but rotten on the inside — illustrates post-traumatic defenses.

Frankel (2017) emphasizes that Ferenczi was precisely the author who showed that the omnipotence found in so-called "mental illnesses" conceals an inexorable fragility and subjective vulnerability; that his

6 "The foetus would much rather remain undisturbed longer in the womb, but it is cruelly turned out into the world […]" (Ferenczi, 1913/1994d, p. 236).

traumatogenesis reveals a failure in the so-called *passive object-love* stage, in which the subject being constituted would need *maternal tenderness* to establish the identifications that would allow him to exercise his authenticity and his desiring motion (Ferenczi, 1933/1994q, p. 163).

Even earlier, since the formulations presented in "Stages in the Development of the Sense of Reality" (Ferenczi, 1913/1994d), pathological fixations were considered to be effects of traumatic disruptions in the omnipotence experience responsible for the expansion of subjectivity that mobilizes the subject from his autoeroticism towards the world, i.e., towards object relations.[7] So, fixation does not only concern a stage of libido development but also the adherence to certain modalities of object relations.

Consequently, it is understood that it is the love received through primary objects that summons the child to object relations, and not life instincts irrespective of the environment, as if such instincts were an autonomous conquest of the subject. The abandoned child, on the other hand, according to Ferenczi (1929/1994m), will be subject to Thanatos. The effect of the traumatic failure in the stage of *passive object-love* would lead to a severe impairment of identification processes, with the consequent incorporation of the object which the subject will no longer be able to do without. Hence the impossibility of mourning the object — and, according to Frankel (2017), the legacy of "omnipotent fantasies".[8]

The clinical challenge posed by narcissistically compromised analysands would not be, therefore, to face the omnipotence arising from the increase in secondary narcissism. On the contrary, it would be caring for the sensitive dimension of the numb subject, so that he can exercise the "delusion" and the "feeling" of primary omnipotence

7 "Introjection", according to Ferenczi (1909/1194a; 1912/1991c).

8 This has led some authors to approximate the splitting described by Ferenczi to the splitting mechanism that characterizes melancholy (*cf.* Pinheiro, 2016; Torok, 1995). However, Freud speaks little of melancholy after his "turning point" of 1920.

(Ferenczi, 1913/1994d, p. 217). Only thus would it be possible to recover the movement of introjection that helps constitute the sphere of the self and the area of objects worthy of the self's desiring investment.

4.4 A clinical approach to masochism

The clinical problem to which Ferenczi especially dedicated himself at the end of his work was that of the *masochism clinic*, which was also a subject of Freud's formulations from 1920 onwards (Birman, 2014a). With the Ferenczian traumatogenesis, the defensive choice of masochism is no longer understood as a "moral cowardice", a refusal of everyday helplessness (Breuer & Freud, 1893–1895/1955, p. 123). The pain caused by identifying with the aggressor would alleviate the greater pain caused by traumatic disavowal, as highlighted by Ferenczi in his *Clinical Diary* (1932/1988, p. 24–31).

In this sense, it can be concluded that the starting point of Ferenczi's concerns was the perception — certainly still intuitive — of the iatrogenic effects of psychoanalysis. The realization that clinical practice in the mid-1910s could reinforce the identification with the aggressor, updated in the figure of the analyst, first led him to the active technique, and then to the creation of what I call an *empathic style*. Effectively, the three-part structure of the free association, the principle of abstinence in the transference, and the interpretation field had been developed for the treatment of neurosis, and not for patients compelled to narcissistic splitting. If we focus on each of the elements that guided the Freudian technique up to 1920, we will see that:

1. Free association did not cause the expected effects, since severe analysands had fragile symbolization processes, and their formations of the unconscious — dreams, slips of the tongue, *Witz* — did not manifest as expected;

2. The frustration caused by the management of transference reproduced less the difference from updated infantile imagos, and more the identification with the aggressor, reinforcing the traumatism and the affective adherence of analysands to their analysts;
3. Interpretation, which targets neurotic resistances and repressed material, was not successful in accessing the analysand's traumatized nucleus, transforming the clinical treatment into an innocuous intellectual exercise, and analyses into interminable experiences. For these subjectivities, insisting on a clinical practice that adopts the acknowledgement of castration as its aim would be the equivalent of putting the cart before the horse, betting on the existence of an (absent) erotic driving force which, on the contrary, would need to be awakened within the relationship with the analyst.

Clinical psychoanalysis then became guided by an ethics of care, based on two main beacons: thalassal regression — which takes us back to the period of tenderness, in which the demand for passive object-love prevails on the part of the analysand — and analysis through game (*cf.* Kupermann, 2017). The term "neocatharsis", conceived by Ferenczi (1930/1994n), comprises both — regression and analysis through game — and indicates the working-through desired by the empathic clinical style developed, with sophistication, in the works of authors such as Balint, Winnicott, and Kohut.

Regression, in this approach, would be the clinical response to the traumatic progression caused by the identification with the aggressor. The sensitive presence of the psychoanalyst would favor the constitution of the necessary and sufficient conditions for the reparative regression of the compromised primary narcissism and for the possibility, for the subject, of finally getting rid of the incorporated object. "[...] behind the submissiveness or even the adoration, just as behind the transference of love [...] there lies hidden an ardent desire to get rid of this oppressive love", writes Ferenczi (1931/1994o, p. 164), adding:

"If we can help the child, the patient [...] to give up the reaction of identification, and to ward off the over-burdening transference, then we may be said to have reached the goal of raising the personality to a higher level".

The concept of analysis through game (Ferenczi, 1931/19940), in turn, aimed to support the expansive and playful movement of analysands who exercise introjection, often through effectively hostile movements — in the sense of trying to expel the aggressor and persecutory object — demanding from the psychoanalyst the availability and strength required to resist *within* the encounter promoted by the field of affectation. The figure of "Aunt Sally", the doll that always comes back to the vertical after being hit by children, is evoked by Ferenczi as an inspiring metaphor for the psychoanalyst's task in certain clinical situations. "The analyst", Ferenczi writes (1928/1994l, p. 95) "like an elastic band, must yield to the patient's pull, but without ceasing to pull in his own direction".

4.5 The principles for an ethics of care in psychoanalysis

In the previous chapter, I showed that a shadow haunts the history of the constitution of psychoanalysis since its origin: the shadow of trauma. In the closing years of the 19th century, Freud devoted himself to comprehending the etiology of neuroses, indicating the traumatic event as the primary cause of their eruption. With the advent of the concepts of fantasy and infantile sexuality, the etiological importance of trauma was reduced, but cases of severe neurosis forced him to resort once again to the traumatic scene — the Wolf Man case study illustrates this movement. After that, impacted by war neurosis and, above all, his theoretical turning point of 1920, Freud developed his second theory of trauma, indicating the death instinct as its elementary factor. Finally, in 1928, Ferenczi undertook his own clinical-theoretical turning point by stressing the obvious: the relationship between adults and children is potentially traumatic, as is the relationship of the subject in a state of vulnerability with the other to whom he directs his request for help and recognition.

Thus, the "Egg of Columbus" presented by Ferenczi to the psychoanalytic community proved that clinical psychology requires the constitution of a very specialized framework for the *care* of those who experience restrictive psychic suffering, which ends up impoverishing their existential experience. If not unanimous, the conception that psychoanalysis is a therapy method guided by an ethics of care is certainly a majority view. An essay by Winnicott from 1952, "Psychoses and Child Care", succeeded in condensing in its title the ultimate importance of environmental care for the constitution of a potent and creative life.

The expansion of the field of action of psychoanalysis to other sectors of society — such as schools, hospitals, and courts of justice — and the presence of psychoanalysts in vulnerable communities, city squares, and streets, or in places where socio-environmental tragedies have happened — helped reinforce the concept that psychoanalytic listening is, essentially, an exercise in caring for others. If some authors (*cf.* Miller, 2011) insist on questioning the psychoanalytic ethics of care, warning of the risk of psychoanalysis being incorporated by a welfare ideal, I believe that, in contemporary times, the greatest risk would be to watch psychoanalysts resist the expansion of psychoanalysis far from the comfort of their consulting rooms, adhering even more to sterilizing orthodoxies.

Over the last decade, a few authors in Brazil, inspired by the environmentalism emphasized by Ferenczi, have dedicated themselves to reflecting on the principles that guide the ethics of care in psychoanalysis (*cf.* Figueiredo, 2009; 2014; *cf.* Maia, 2009; *cf.* Rocha, 2011; 2013). Our objective in this chapter, following these and other efforts, is to contribute to a metapsychology of care based on the three pillars of Ferenczi's work: the theory of subjective constitution and the advent of language, clinical theory, and metapsychology of the psychoanalyst's psychic processes.

In reading carefully, the reader will notice that each of the *times of trauma* that I propose calls for one of the principles of the ethics of care in psychoanalysis — hospitality, empathy, and the analyst's health. Thus, the *time of the unspeakable* requires the psychoanalyst to show the necessary *hospitality* to take on those who cannot express in words the decisive experiences of their suffering; the *time of testimony* requires the psychoanalyst to have the *empathy* that will allow him to hear, feel, and witness the pain that was silenced by the analysand; lastly, the *time of disavowal* requires the psychoanalyst's *health,* which is indispensable for him to offer his sensitive presence in the face of the horror imposed by traumatic repetition.

4.5.1 The principle of hospitality

Returning to the central argument developed by Ferenczi in "The Adaptation of the Family to the Child", the newborn's bio-psycho-physiological dependence, named by Freud as a "state of helplessness" (*Hilflosigkeit*), originates from the fact that the child's relationship with adults can be effectively traumatic. The problem of adaptation thus gains a new color, as it is now considered a two-way operation in which the primary adaptation — preventing the birth and cultural insertion of the *infans* from causing or being experienced as a trauma — is that of the environment that welcomes the new child, not the other way around, which is of course why we use the term "Ferenczian environmentalism".

Indeed, if, in Ferenczi's words (1928/1994k, p. 64), "for none of the developments and changes which life brings was the individual so well prepared as for birth", this is because "physiology and the instincts of the parents go to make this transition as smooth as possible".

On the one hand, the lungs and the heart are well formed; on the other hand, parents are compelled to offer maximum comfort to the newborn. For Ferenczi, the greatest difficulties in existing do not lie in the state of helplessness that is characteristic of the human being, but in the modes of socialization to which children are submitted in their path of insertion in a certain cultural context, capable of creating a morbid "confusion" in which "what the parents do not comprehend is precisely what the children understand only too well and experience deeply, and what the children cannot fathom is as clear as daylight to the parents" (Ferenczi, 1928/1994k, p. 69).

In the year following the publication of "The Adaptation of the Family to the Child", Ferenczi dedicated his time to writing "The Unwelcome Child and His Death Instinct" (1929/1994m), which can be considered its clinical development. It is an argument supported by case studies of patients with psychosomatic symptoms and suicidal tendencies, which anticipates his traumatogenesis. Referring to some of these cases, Ferenczi (1929/1994m, p. 103–104) states: "Both patients came into the world as *unwelcome guests of the family* [...] their desire to live had been weakened [...]".

Thus, an unwelcome child is one who is confronted with a hostile environment, insensitive to his/her needs, in which he/she is *persona non grata.* To explore what it would mean to be an unwelcome guest in the context of Ferenczi's discussion, we can get a closer view of his perspective in an approximation of the two apparently little-connected concepts. This view is based on experiences of the elasticity of psychoanalytic technique.

In the first place, suspending the requirement of associative effort for analysands who were previously considered impossible to analyze would allow them, according to Ferenczi, "to enjoy the irresponsibility of childhood" for the first time. Furthermore, for a patient with diminished pleasure in living, it would be effectively necessary to promote an "introduction of positive life impulses and motives for his subsequent existence", which would be equivalent to "supplying [...] *tenderness*" also in the context of the transference encounter (1929/1994m, p. 106–107). Consequently, it is argued, that the experience of tenderness and the possibility of enjoying the irresponsibility of childhood are closely related — the latter being, in fact, a consequence of the former.

As seen in Chapter 3, tenderness acquires a conceptual status in the final period of Ferenczi's work, referring to his understanding of the traumatic event. The subtitle of the famous essay "Confusion of Tongues between Adults and the Child", from 1933, is "The Language of Tenderness and Passion".[9] Ferenczi believes this refers to a precocious erotic experience, which we can even describe as primary: that of being loved in the stage of passive object-love, i.e., before the possibility of any differentiation between the self and the other, such as can help to integrate the instances of the ego. The experience of tenderness would thus be the condition for the possibility of an expansive exercise of introjection, and even for the constitution of primary narcissism and the Freudian pleasure-ego.

The enjoyment of the "irresponsibility of childhood", in turn, would mean the possibility to experience the "illusion of omnipotence", or "feeling of omnipotence", arising from the "animist period" in the child's apprehension of reality. However, these ideas will only become intelligible when referencing the notions presented years earlier in "Stages in the Development of the Sense of Reality", from 1913, which expresses Ferenczi's attempt to comprehend the interplay between the pleasure principle and the reality principle, which had recently been described by Freud (1911/1980h).

---

9 The German term for tenderness found in the original version is *Zärtlichkeit*, which refers to both the display of affection and the care given to someone you love (Ferenczi, 1933/1994p).

4.5.1.1 Sexualization of the universe, symbolization, and the advent of language

Ferenczi establishes the origin of the pleasure principle by postulating a mythical "period of unconditional omnipotence" (Ferenczi, 1913/1994d, p. 233) experienced by the fetus in the mother's womb, which the subject would regressively seek to re-create and re-experience throughout his existence. Omnipotence, defined as "the feeling that one has all that one wants, and that one has nothing left to wish for" (Ferenczi, 1913/1994d, p. 219), would simultaneously be the genesis and the desired destination of the pleasure principle.

As Freud (1950[1895]/1966b; 1900/1980d; 1900/1980e) had demonstrated, after birth, the experience of satisfaction provided by the mother's breast would inaugurate the hallucinatory thinking that, as revised by Ferenczi (Ferenczi, 1913/1994d, p. 221), would represent the "hallucinatory re-occupation" of the lost intrauterine state of satisfaction. With success in adaptation to the environment, the child would enter the "period of magical hallucinatory omnipotence" (Ferenczi, 1913/1994d, p. 223), since the hallucinated object would be effectively present when necessary, satisfying his needs and fulfilling his desires. Even after overcoming this period, we would daily regress to it in our night dreams; its pathological equivalent — a sign of fixation at this stage — would be a psychotic hallucination.

Over time, the "external world" would no longer respond promptly to the baby's hallucinatory movements, who would thus have to perform "motor work" to provide clues of his demands to caregivers. It is true that, from the beginning, motor discharges accompanied by crying were signified by the mother as vital and met needs. According to Ferenczi, the *infans* quickly learns to symbolize his yearnings through "corresponding gestures" (Ferenczi, 1913/1994d, p. 225): imitating suction movements to be fed, abdominal sounds, and contractions to have his diapers changed, and, more elaborately, pointing to the objects he covets, constituting a "veritable gesture-language" (Ferenczi, 1913/1994d, p. 225) capable of expressing the increasing complexity of his desires. This would be the "period of omnipotence with the help of magic gestures". When this stage is overcome, the belief in superstitious gestures, such as religious blessings or even joining our hands to pray, would survive in our daily lives. On the other hand, in social life, body rituals — such as dance in traditional cultures or sorcery — as well as our pleasure in stage magic performances, would also be an expression of this stage. The pathological equivalent of this period, in turn, would be recognizable in "hysterical conversion", understood since Freud as a neurotic mode of wish-fulfillment.

In the process of psychic maturation, two forces will contribute to the overcoming of this second stage of the development of the sense of reality. On the one hand, the intensification of needs and the complexity of "his ever more *audacious* wishes" will force the child to submit to new conditions to see them satisfied (Ferenczi, 1913/1994d, p. 226). On the other hand, an "invincible hostile power" — the other, the adult caregiver — may not respond to it, or may even oppose it. At that moment, the distinction between the self and the external world would effectively be established. It reads: "Till now the 'all-powerful' being has been able to feel himself one with the world that obeyed him and followed his every nod, but gradually there appears a painful discordance in his experiences" (Ferenczi, 1913/1994d, p. 226). However, not even this objectivization of the world "does not at once destroy every tie between the ego and the non-ego" (Ferenczi, 1913/1994d, p. 227). The child will resort to the establishment of "symbolic representation" (Ferenczi, 1913/1994d, p. 228), which, as in the animist period that characterized the evolution of the species, perceives the world as a reproduction of his corporeality. In this way, the same gesture that establishes the self/other distinction becomes responsible, through animistic thinking, for creating devices capable of influencing these "'divine' powers" (Ferenczi, 1913/1994d, p. 229) on which he depends to fulfill his desires.

At that moment, the most powerful instrument to influence the other and transform reality emerges: language. Ferenczi writes: "Speech symbolism thus gets substituted for gesture symbolism" (Ferenczi, 1913/1994d, p. 229), and the child has access to the "period of magic thoughts and magic words" (Ferenczi, 1913/1994d, p. 230). In Ferenczi's conception, though, language would be in origin an "imitation" through which sounds and noises are reproduced, and a sequence of sounds is established in a "close associative connection with definite objects and processes" (Ferenczi, 1913/1994d, p. 229). *A particular case, therefore, of the symbolic relations arising from the perception of the child's own corporeality.*

According to Jô Gondar (2017, p. 115), in Ferenczi's conception of language as mimesis "one goes from the sensible to the meaning, and not from the signifier to the meaning". Language thus acquires an evocative function, with the power to present the world, signaling the expansive movement of subjectivity towards the encounter with significant objects. "The word", continues Gondar, "expresses more than it signifies, makes present more than it represents" (Gondar, 2017, p. 119).

In two essays specifically addressing the process that constitutes symbolic relations, Ferenczi (1913/1992a; 1913/1994c) reiterates his conception of a corporeal origin of the creation of symbols. Initially, he argues, the child's psyche is exclusively interested in sensations of satisfaction and enjoyment originating from his erogenous zones, referring to the functions of food absorption or excretion. From these very experiences, his attention would be drawn to the things and processes in the world that refer him to the erogenous body. In his words:

> *This is how these deep relationships that persist throughout life are established between the human body and the world of*

> *objects, which we call symbolic relationships. At this stage, the child only sees in the world reproductions of his corporeality, while also learning to represent, through his body, all the diversity of the external world. This is how the "sexualization of the universe" manifests itself (1913/1992a, p. 107).*

An example offered by Ferenczi (1913/1992a, p. 107) is quite illustrative of his understanding of the evocative power of language. An 18-month-old, seeing the Danube for the first time, exclaims: "So much spit!" The joy expressed by this utterance is evident, evoking the creative power of the instinctual subject, which is the meaning of the feeling of omnipotence proposed by Ferenczi as the driving force that leads the subject from hallucinatory thought to the magic gesture, and from there to the use of the word, with no traumatic disruption in the process of acquiring a sense of reality.

It is interesting to notice that the embryo of these formulations is to be found in the child's exploration of the function of the use of obscene words, which begins in the latency phase. For Ferenczi (1911/1994b),[10] the enthusiasm for obscene words resides in the fact that they "possess the capacity of compelling the hearer to revive memory pictures in a *regressive and hallucinatory manner*"; and in the one who enunciates them, to rescue the intimate connection between word and act. Precisely for this reason, it could be concluded that obscene words "have attributes which all words must have possessed in some early stage of psychical development". Ferenczi thus refers to a "concreteness, and with it probably a strong tendency to regression, applies still to all words" at a certain stage of development (Ferenczi, 1911/1994b, p. 137–140).

10 Evidently inspired by Freud's book (1905/1980g) on the *Witz*, translated as *Jokes and their Relation to the Unconscious*.

With this, Ferenczi approximates the hallucinatory and even regressive dimension of obscene words, as well as the intimacy with motricity and act that certain words have the ability to evoke, to the "mother tongue" (Ferenczi, 1911/1994b, p. 137–140). Elsewhere, I demonstrate how the mother tongue refers, also in Freud's work, to an incarnated word endowed with the power of self-expressiveness and affectation of the other (*cf.* Kupermann, 2003, Chapter 6). The novelty that Ferenczi presents us, which contains the germ of his greatest intuitions, is the *transposition to clinical practice* of the Freudian formulations (and even intuitions) present in *Jokes and Their Relation to the Unconscious*; a task which effectively neither Freud nor any other psychoanalyst of subsequent generations undertook.

Consequently, Ferenczi's suggestion (1911/1994b) that it would be up to the psychoanalyst to explicitly "authorize" the analysand to use the forbidden words that came into his mind already reveals the distinctive characteristic of his clinical practice: so that free association — and its developments in the form of repetitions and acting-out — could actually occur, it would be necessary for the psychoanalyst to contribute to the creation of a favorable space for speaking; this is the meaning of *laisser-faire*, the elasticity of technique, and the relaxation principle. Psychoanalysis would therefore be a true exercise to "loosen [...] their tongues" (*cf.* Ferenczi, 1933/1994q, p. 166), favoring the possibility of using the magic and evocative word, the *poietic* language capable of creating a sense of self and of the world.

Thus, the notion of a "language of tenderness", proper to the child, which tends to confuse the universe of adults, presented in the last essay published by Ferenczi (1933), has its embryo in the period of magic thoughts and words of the development of a sense of reality, configuring an eroticized word capable of sexualizing the universe and creating for itself the field of objects worthy of its libidinal investments. The language of tenderness is at once delicate and *louche*, tender and obscene, heir to the polymorphous perversity that characterizes the pre-genital stages of libido development. Its use involves recovering the "exuberance" of the life drive and of "playfulness", through which the omnipotent child evokes objects that can serve the purposes of his desires (Ferenczi, 1913/1994c, p. 275).

For Ferenczi, the psychoanalytic clinic — the space, *par excellence*, of our modern world in which the subject is called upon to use the word with its full evocative function — needs to be governed by the rule of hospitality towards the *infans*, the one who cannot speak… outside the language of tenderness.

To encounter a definition of "unconditional hospitality" as given to the foreigner (or outsider), the philosopher Jacques Derrida was inspired by the trial of Socrates. Of special interest to us is how he defines the condition of a "foreigner", which becomes a revealing analogy for the challenges of the work that clinical psychoanalysis aims to do.

To the court that will judge him, Socrates gives a speech that reveals the essential core of the condition of a "foreigner". He justifies the inadequacy of his words by saying that he feels completely foreign to the language of the courts and that he only knows how to express himself in the language he usually uses in the public square, where he teaches. From these words, Derrida (2000) infers the definition of "foreigner" as someone who does not speak the language of those to whom he addresses his request for shelter:

> *if he was already speaking our language, with all that that implies, if we already shared everything that is shared with a language, would the foreigner still be a foreigner and could we speak of asylum or hospitality in regard to him? This is the paradox […] (Derrida, 2000, p. 15–17)*

The discussion established by Derrida on hospitality and the condition of the foreigner can help us follow Ferenczi in his reading that some analysands who were under intense suffering, with psychosomatic symptoms and even suicidal tendencies, would have been *unwelcome guests of the family*. The question of hospitality would thus be expanded from the geopolitical context — in which it might be restricted to, for example, the drastic situation of refugees — to the human condition itself. This is because each of us experiences, at the moment we arrive in the world as *infans*, the challenge of the paradox demonstrated by Derrida: being recognized in the human community even before we speak the language we are destined to adopt, which would legitimize our belonging to a given culture. Consequently, the reading of "The Unwelcome Child and His Death Instinct" allows us to state that *we are all foreigners in search of asylum and hospitality*.

The hospitality principle would therefore impose itself as the first principle of the ethics of care in psychoanalysis. In a psychoanalytical space guided by the empathic style, the analysand will find the opportunity to create, with the analyst, by exercising the language of tenderness, words capable of evoking the sense of his singularity.

For this to happen, however, the psychoanalyst must be able to refrain from any tendency to the interpretative excess that aims to talk *about* the child that inhabits each analysand. His challenge becomes to talk *to* the child, promoting the analytical space to the shared game space that produces meaning.

4.5.2 The principle of empathy

The team of Coq Héron, who were responsible for the translation of the works of Ferenczi into French, made the curious choice of a musical metaphor to refer to the field of affects which comes into being between the partners in the clinical experience. In the French edition, we read, in the final paragraphs of "Elasticité de la technique psychanalytique":

> *The procedure which I apply and recommend, elasticity, is certainly not equivalent to giving in without resistance. We seek, in fact, to place ourselves* in tune with *the patient — as if we were a* tuning-fork — *to feel with him all his whims, all his moods, but also we remain tied firmly to our position dictated by the analytical experience (Ferenczi, 1928/1982 p. 64).*[11]

As we know, the tuning fork — the expression used to refer to the magnitude of the patient's feelings — is the artifact that resonates at a pitch to allow for the tuning of instruments, thus enabling the harmony of a musical ensemble. According to what we read in Ferenczi, it is the patient, unequivocally, who sets the tone (the mood) that composes the atmosphere of the clinical encounter; his time, and his pace.

Freud, apparently, was not a music lover; more accustomed to the laws of grammar, he preferred literature (*cf.* Gay, 1989). He did, though, use an analogy years earlier — certainly less musical — that may have served as an inspiration for Ferenczi and some of his successors: the psychoanalyst "must turn his own unconscious like a receptive organ towards the transmitting unconscious of the patient. He must adjust himself to the patient as a telephone receiver is adjusted to the transmitting microphone" (Freud, 1912/1958a, p. 115–116).

After the initial surprise, it is possible to understand the use of musical metaphors and sound analogies to refer to the range of modes of interaction between analyst and analysand, as an opening stage of the clinical activity, beyond listening to the strict sphere of the word and, in counterpart, beyond the psychoanalyst's interpretation. Sensitive allegories have, indeed, imposed themselves as a critique of the dominant use of interpretation, and as an indication that the

11 In the original German, and in the translation into English, curiously, the reference to a tuning fork does not appear (*cf.* Ferenczi, 1928/1994l; 1928/1939).

analytic experience entails an unrepentant aesthetic dimension that, if disregarded, risks compromising all possibilities of treatment.

Freud did not fail to observe this evidence and, quite early in his work, criticized the violence of interpretive excess. In the essay that can be considered the "flagship" of his writings on technique, "Wild Psychoanalysis", he exemplified (in a rather cartoonish way, as the reader will see) how a *tactless* interpretation carries traumatogenic potential. He had written (Freud, 1910/1957a) that an abrupt interpretation, which does not consider transference and resistances, has the same effect on the analysand as "a distribution of menu-cards in a time of famine has upon hunger", meaning that it would be innocuous. He wrote (p. 226) that "medical tact", looked upon as "a special gift" and "indefinable", equips the psychoanalyst to assess the appropriateness of an intervention. This was, certainly, the first time that Freud employed an aesthetic reference in describing clinical practice — and, indeed, precisely in the context of the presentation of the works that became known as his essays on psychoanalytic technique. The problem is that far from being harmless (as the gastronomic illustration might suggest), abrupt interpretation is effectively iatrogenic.

In "The Elasticity of Psycho-Analytic Technique", Ferenczi (1928/1994l) returns to the notion of clinical tact to introduce a much more radical concept: the concept of empathy (*Einfühlung*). According to Ferenczi, his main motivation in writing the essay was to complement Freud's "technical writings", in which, as the master himself confessed in a letter dated January 4th, 1928 (*apud* Pigman, 1995, p. 132–133), much emphasis was placed on what the psychoanalyst should *not* do, leaving "almost every positive thing that should be done to tact". Thus, at that moment in Ferenczi's work and also in the construction of the psychoanalysis field, it was a question of removing from the category of "tact" its "mystical" — "special" and "indefinable" — element.

Ferenczi believed that the notion that for the success or failure of an analysis the "personal equation" or "personal note" of the psychoanalyst, i.e., his talent, prevailed, would cease to be effective as analysts went through a psychoanalytic training process, in which personal analysis was a *sine qua non* condition; which, since the Bad-Homburg congress of 1925, had become the norm in the psychoanalytic movement (I will return to this point later). Well-analyzed psychoanalysts would have more access to their blind spots and unconscious tendencies and greater sensitive availability for the management required by movements of transference. Although excessively optimistic, his project of honing, through adequate training, the sensitivity of those who wish to take care of human suffering is nevertheless stimulating.

Following this train of argument, "psychological tact" would consist of the exercise of certain faculties guided by the psychoanalyst's sensitivity. Thus, it is a matter of

> *whether or when one should tell the patient some particular thing, when the material he has produced should be considered sufficient to draw conclusions [...] when one should keep silent [...] and at what point the further maintenance of silence would result only in causing the patient useless suffering. (Ferenczi, 1928/1994l, p. 89)*

In sum, Ferenczi declares: "It is the capacity for empathy" (*Ferenczi, 1928b, p. 89*).

The German term *Einfühlung*, usually translated as empathy, literally means *feeling within*, not "feeling with".[12] Chaim Katz (2009) suggests the understanding that, in the case of the psychoanalytic experience, it would not be a matter of projection or identification (in the Freudian

---

12 In the French translation there is the phrase "*Le tact, c'est la faculté de sentir avec*", with the German term in the footnotes (Ferenczi, 1928/1982, p. 55); but in the original German version (the essay was published in the *Internationale Zeitschrift für Psychoanalyse* in 1928) there is the phrase "*Takt ist Einfühlungsvermögen*", without any reference to sympathy, or "feeling with" (Ferenczi, 1928/1939, p. 383).

sense), but of the psychoanalyst's ability to feel the analysand within himself, which implies the availability to *become* another.

4.5.2.1 An enlightened romantic

The term *Einfühlung* is imported from romantic aesthetics of the 18th and 19th centuries and appears in Freudian writings as early as in *Jokes and Their Relation to the Unconscious*. According to Pigman (1995), however, commentators on Freud did not give it due importance: neither with regard to the processes of affective contagion, which takes place in theatrical staging, and in *Witz* in particular, nor with regard to its importance for romantic aesthetes.

Philosopher Theodor Lipps, an important representative of the *Einfühlungsästhetik* and widely quoted by Freud, developed a theory of unconscious imitation based on the perception of facial mimicry, to explain how we have access to feelings experienced and not verbalized by another person (Koeppel, 1990). Indeed, empathy does have an uncomfortable proximity not only to the field of imitation, but also to phenomena considered to come from mysticism, such as intuition, occult phenomena, and telepathic communication.

Freud had not failed to alert Ferenczi to the risk of some analysts relying on references to the sensitive elements of clinical practice to justify their arbitrariness. Nevertheless, he recognized the importance of removing the "mystical" element from the notion of tact. Quite recently, to the astonishment of part of the psychoanalytic community, French psychoanalyst Laurence Kahn (2014) published a veritable manifesto against "empathic analysts", accusing them — especially those representing relational psychoanalysis in the United States, and those who believe the importance of the analyst's countertransference-affects in the direction of the treatment — of underestimating the rigor and importance of Freudian metapsychology, as well as the guiding principles of the interpretive technique in psychoanalysis. Ferenczi himself (1928/1994l) did not fail to point out that some analysts might interpret his proposition of elasticity as a "masochistic technique", similarly to how the active technique had been adopted as an alibi for analysts to "indulge their tendency to impose on their patients entirely unanalytic rules, which sometimes border on sadism" (p. 100).

The fact that the analytic experience can turn into a sadomasochistic exercise should no longer be surprising (*cf.* Kupermann, 2014b). What is impressive is the persistent resistance on the part of the psychoanalytic field — after almost a century since the admission of the complexity that permeates the exercise of contemporary science — to acknowledging a phenomenon that pertains to subjective constitution and intersubjective interaction, due to the simple fact that it questions the sovereignty of individuality, evoking an inexorable (and undesirable) constitutive *mixture* between the fields of the self and the other.

In recent research on empathy, Bartholomeu Vieira (2017) demonstrated how Freud occupied a hybrid position concerning the scientific culture of his time, combining the positivist rationality, typical of the Enlightenment, with the interest in the dark areas of knowledge propagated by Romanticism. Encouraged by Ferenczi, and by his daughter Anna, Freud (1941[1921]/1980q; 1922/1980k) even explored (albeit timidly) the phenomena of telepathy. His taste for paradox, situations that skew from equilibrium, and impure phenomena led Yirmiyahu Yovel (1993) to rightly nickname Freud as a "dark enlightenment thinker".

Inverting Yovel's formula, we could say that Ferenczi, due to his appreciation for the anomalous phenomena that can come up in psychoanalytic clinical practice, was an *enlightened romantic*: while he closely followed Freud's efforts to provide psychoanalysis with a scientific grounding, he insisted on questioning, in the name of the work of the affects, the limits of psychoanalytic rationalism.

The very formulation of an "elasticity of technique" — an oxymoron in itself — almost took the form of a criticism of the interpretive style, and of the guiding principles of psychoanalytic clinical practice, with an emphasis on criticism of the principle of abstinence, and of the psychoanalyst's neutrality. However, as Eliana Schueler Reis and Jô Gondar (2017, p. 14) observe, "mixture is not fusion"; we could posit that mixture is a mimesis comprising the self and the world of objects and entails the possibility of transit and alternation between the territories of the self and the other.

4.5.2.2 Empathy and introjection

A year after his first personal encounter with Freud, Ferenczi published an essay that would impact the psychoanalytic field; not only because of the anticipation of many ideas that would be taken up by Freud years later (such as transference, hypnosis, and the role of the father complex in therapeutic power in general), but, above all, because of the presentation of his original conception of subjective constitution. The essay is "Introjection and Transference" (1909/1994a). His motivation was to demonstrate that the condition for psychoanalytic transference resides in a more elementary and universal process, which Ferenczi names introjection — the primary movement from autoeroticism towards objects (*cf.* Landa, 1999).

However, to understand the originality of the concept of introjection one needs to consider both what Freud had presented before 1909, and what Ferenczi would outline years later, especially regarding the mechanisms of constitution of symbolic relationships, to which I referred above.

Starting with the idea that "to the new-born child everything perceived by the senses appears unitary, so to speak monistic" (Ferenczi, 1909/1994a, p. 48), i.e., without any differentiation from the object, Ferenczi suggests, based on the Freudian notion of autoeroticism, that the experiences that matter initially are those resulting from sensations of pleasure, which he calls "subjective physical contents" (*Gefühl*) (Ferenczi, 1913/1994d, p. 226). Hence, he can say that "in the beginning the child only likes satiety, because it appeases the hunger that tortures him — later he ends up also liking the mother, that object that gives him satiety". Using his hypotheses about the stages of development of the sense of reality, we could say that the dominance of "subjective physical contents" would coincide with the periods in which the child experiences "omnipotence", and a complete lack of discrimination between himself and the environment.

In 1912, Ferenczi wrote a short essay entitled "On the Definition of Introjection", in an attempt to clarify his formulation. It reads: "I described introjection as an extension to the external world of the original autoerotic interests, by including its objects in the ego" (Ferenczi, 1912/1991c, p. 316).

The reader who is more familiar with the Freudian text will be able to see the "pseudopods" of the greedy amoeba presented in the essay on narcissism. After all, there is, in fact, a libidinal impulse to search for objects that can function as a sign of the constitutive insufficiency of the instinctual body.[13]

The novelty of 1912 is that Ferenczi points to a movement that starts from autoeroticism towards the object world, not necessarily mediated by the narcissistic unity — thus insisting on its primordial monism. Further on, we read: "I conceive the mechanism of all transference on to an object, that is to say all kinds of object love, as introjection, as extension of the ego" (Ferenczi, 1912/1991c, p. 317). However, how should we understand this condition of indiscernibility between self and other, subject and object, proposed by Ferenczi? The resumption

13 Ferenczi uses the term *Süchtigkeit,* yearning, to refer to the property of the "free floating" libido that is always unsatisfied in search of objects, the source of introjection (Ferenczi, 1909/1994a, p. 84).

of his theory of symbolization — in which bodily sensations would be the matrix of symbolic object relations — comes to our aid.

As an illustration, let us take a look at Ferenczi's understanding of the *infans*' interest in his excrement, considered intermediate objects between the self and the world: "part of himself, a transitional (*Zwischending*) something between him and his environment, i.e. between subject and object" (Ferenczi, 1928/1994k, p. 67). Here, one can evoke the everyday example of babies who, when crawling, spread their vomit on the floor, or even the child mentioned by Ferenczi who, upon seeing the Danube, exclaims "So much spit!". Symbolic relations, understood as an extension of the erogenous body, would be, therefore, a particular case of introjection. The "*introjection phase*" refers to the primordial stage, "since in it all experiences are still incorporated into the ego" *(cf.* Ferenczi, 1913/1994d, p. 227), *to which one returns throughout life, each time a spontaneous creative gesture is expressed.*

With maturation, the child will be forced to acknowledge the "maliciousness of things" — the gradual resistance of objects to yield to his will — and, consequently, displeasure. So, the "first projection process" or the "primordial projection" (Ferenczi, 1909/1994a, p. 48) will emerge, through which objects (associated with displeasure) are excluded from the mass of perceptions that henceforth constitute his ego. Primitive projection would be the condition for the emergence of the "objectified [physical contents]" (*Empfindung*) (Ferenczi, 1913/ 1994d, p. 226). "Monism becomes dualism", but the stages of omnipotence — which the subject resorts to in his perpetual process of establishing symbolic relationships with the object world — should be understood as "introjection phases". The "*projection phase*" would be "the later one" (*cf.* Ferenczi, 1913/1994d, p. 226–227).

It is worth noting that Freud, in his metapsychological essay on the vicissitudes of the drive, had formulated an original "Reality-ego" pertaining to the autoerotic stage that, despite being prior to the pleasure-ego arising from primary narcissism, would carry the seed of the singular feeling of self. Paradoxically, it is an Ego affected by the sensations provoked by the encounter with the other, and the perception of a differentiation concerning that same other would come later (Freud, 1915/1957b, p. 134). Despite not expanding the status of his recently formulated *original reality-ego* throughout his work, Freud admits to having been inspired by Ferenczi's notion of introjection, in which the sensational, autoerotic subject — of instinctual origin, therefore — would be subjected to a permanent movement of extension to the world of objects, not due to a constitutive lack, but due to an "exuberance", initially corporeal, as Ferenczi (1913/1994c) would say, seeking sensations.

Going back to our central problem, the principle of empathy as an element of the ethics of care in psychoanalysis: if the 1909 essay had been written by Ferenczi at a later time, its title would probably not be "Introjection and Transference", but "Introjection and Empathy". If it is the case that transference should serve to designate the introjections that manifest themselves in the course of analysis, then with the turning point of 1928 these introjections would be better understood in the light of empathy, a more primal phenomenon and, at the same time, more complex than transference as understood in its Freudian sense (the analysand's infantile unconscious *imagos* updated in the figure of the psychoanalyst). More than *updating* the infantile unconscious *imagos*, empathy refers to *production by the unconscious* through the affective encounter established between analyst and analysand.

Empathy is closely related to the "union" between the *self* and the objects that characterize the introjection that constitutes subjectivity. It reveals the insufficiency we are faced with every time we seek to define the subject in reference to his individuality; it points to our psychical permeability, which comes into play every time we make ourselves available to the exercise of affectation that is superimposed on the transferential space in analysis. Like music that fills a given environment, though often unnoticed, empathy creates an intermediate space, a bridge that favors the constitution of a "field of affectation" (Maia, 2004) between the partners in the clinical experience, allowing the analyst to have aesthetic access to the analysand's unconscious, often without the need for it to be expressed in words.

Perla Klautau Pimentel and Nelson Coelho Junior (2009) demonstrated three aspects of empathy in the clinic: it is simultaneously a sensitive "listening mode", through which the psychoanalyst can access the psychic states of his analysand; a "form of communication", often quiet, but which also includes the intonation, volume and rhythm of the psychoanalyst's words; and a "therapeutic factor" in itself, due to the fact that, for the analysand, the empathic experience provides a form of mirroring and recognition that acquires the meaning of unconditional hospitality.

In the April 12, 1932 entry of the *Clinical Diary*, there are two comments that may illustrate the importance given by Ferenczi to empathy in his clinical style (1932/1988, p. 84–86). In the first, while self-criticizing his attitude towards a patient, Ferenczi writes: "Instead of feeling with the heart, I feel with my head. Head and thought replace heart and libido". As such, for the possibility of therapeutic effectiveness in some analyses, there would be "that little 'something'" missing, which was empathy. Further on, we read: "Ultimately I meant by this that when two people converse, not only a conscious dialogue takes place but an unconscious one, from both sides". This occurs because "the transference relationship could quite significantly promote the development of subtler manifestations of receptivity".

For Ferenczi, only the analyst's analysis, acting on his resistances, can ensure access to empathic sensitivity, overcoming resistances and the "obtuseness of the analyst" (Ferenczi, 1932/1988, p. 84–86).

4.5.3 The principle of the analyst's health

In "The Elasticity of Psychoanalytic Technique", Ferenczi formulates the need to conceive a "second fundamental rule" of psychoanalysis, the analysis of the analyst, in line with the fundamental rule of free association posited by Freud in his technical writings. It appears that, for Ferenczi, the condition for free association to occur is, rather, that the analyst has been analyzed, which would lead us to assume that, in fact, the analyst's analysis would be the *first* rule, not the second, for any analysis to take place.

But what is the need, in 1928, for an author of Ferenczi's standing to emphasize so eloquently the imperative for the analyst to undergo analysis? After all, since the International Bad-Homburg Congress in 1925, "training analysis" became a requirement in psychoanalytic training institutes (*cf.* Kupermann, 2014b). It might be assumed that his intention was to underline the new rule, so as to dilute any resistance to it, which does make sense. However, a stronger hypothesis, supported by the third essay of the trilogy that makes up the turning point of 1928, "The Problem of the Termination of the Analysis", is that Ferenczi intended to criticize the so-called training analyses in advance for the fact that they complied with institutional standards and regulations, considering that the analysis of analysts, more than any others, should be taken up to termination and completed.[14]

I also believe that three other reasons led Ferenczi to formulate the second fundamental rule: first, the empathic clinical style proposed since the turning point of 1928 demanded great sensitive availability from the psychoanalyst, and an in-depth analysis would be the best way to attain it; second, there was Ferenczi's evident dissatisfaction with the treatment undertaken with Freud and, as a result, his own demand for

14 Ferenczi's influence on Lacan (1968/2003) is explicit in the conception — which gave origin to Lacan's concept of the "pass" — that the analysand can become an analyst, as an effect of the termination of his analysis.

analysis; and finally, his perception that the main resistances to analysis derive from the resistances of the psychoanalyst.

Let us look at each of these claims in detail.

In an entry in the *Clinical Diary* on June 3, 1932, entitled "No special training analysis!", Ferenczi questions both training analyses and training supervisions of analysts in training, stating that analysts should be better analyzed than their patients, but were in fact "analyzed worse" — and that this needed to be corrected by "repeated supplementary analyses". After all, he had already concluded that "the best analyst is a patient who has been cured". Finally, we read a warning: "*No attempts to defend oneself*" from the criticism of analysands, who complain that they do not recognize "any relaxation" in the practice of their analysts (1932/1988, p. 115).

The curious thing is that Ferenczi can be considered the creator, in the 1910s, of training analysis. It was his initiative to determine that members of the "secret committee" — which brought together Freud's closest disciples — should undergo analysis with the master, to transmit the "pure theory unadulterated by personal complexes", avoiding new traumatic rifts such as with Adler and Jung (Grosskurth, 1991, p. 46). However, especially after the turning point of 1928, Ferenczi would become a relentless critic not only of the interpretive style in the clinic but also of the institutionalization process of the psychoanalytic movement, which adopted the model proposed by Berlin as a paradigm, contributing to his being dubbed the *enfant terrible* of psychoanalysis (Ferenczi, 1931/19940, p. 127).

One example lies in the requirement for supervision (referred to as "control analysis" at the time). While the Hungarians, led by Ferenczi, believed that supervision, understood above all as an analysis of countertransference, should be carried out by the analyst of the candidate in training, the Berlin group, led by Eitingon, had suggested that supervision be carried out with another psychoanalyst so that the candidate had the opportunity to broaden his references. Yet, according to Balint (1948) — Ferenczi's intellectual heir — the hidden reason was that if the supervisor was not the same person as the psychoanalyst, he would not be subject to analytic rules and would therefore feel more comfortable expressing his own convictions, points of view, and theoretical preferences, which would more successfully carry out the "esoteric objective" of standard psychoanalytic training: to instruct, and even reprimand, candidates in training, establishing a true "superegoic training" that promotes obedience (Balint, 1948, p. 167–171).

Ferenczi, on the other hand, believed that the course of an analysis should produce precisely the opposite: "it is the business of a real character analysis to do away [...] with any kind of super-ego, including that of the analyst. [...] Only a complete dissolution of the super-ego can bring about a radical cure" (1928/1994l, p. 98).

On this basis, incorporation of the superego which, according to Balint (1948), takes place in training analyses would then be a move in the opposite direction to what would properly be expected from psychoanalytic training.

Effectively, an analysis that promotes the incorporation of superego nuclei — through their identification to the analyst — becomes traumatogenic, bringing the transference experience closer to an identification with the aggressor. For Ferenczi, the formula by which the analysand needs to get rid of the superego does not mean to deprive the subject of his ideals, but rather to free him from the tyranny of the unconscious superego, that which cannot be influenced. Consequently, the analysand "will no longer have to obey his preconscious super-ego so slavishly as he had previously to obey his unconscious parent imago" (Ferenczi, 1928/1994l, p. 101).

In the *Clinical Diary*, as well as the criticism that Freud had not paid attention to his negative transference (addressed in Chapter 1), we find Ferenczi recording a painful testimony about his own analysis:

> *My own analysis could not be pursued deeply enough because my analyst (by his own admission, of a narcissistic nature), with his strong determination to be healthy and his antipathy toward any weaknesses or abnormalities, could not follow me down into those depths, and introduced the "educational" stage too soon (1932/1988, p. 62)*

The question of the analyst's health appears in this passage not as something desired, but as a criticism of the defenses employed by the analyst (Freud, in this case). Preserving "good health" would entail distancing oneself from the patients' suffering (their "weaknesses" and "anomalies"), keeping their narcissism intact; precisely the opposite of what is advocated by the empathic style, in which the psychoanalyst offers himself for the affective encounter with the analysand — the only way, indeed, to affect the analysand with inferences, interpretations, constructions, and even a significant silence. "Analysis demands of the physician, not only a firm control of his own narcissism but also a sharp watch on his emotional reactions of every kind" (1928/1994l, p. 95).

In an extremely provocative way, Ferenczi resorts to caricature to criticize the attitude of coldness and indifference caused by a bad reading of Freud's technical recommendations. It would be impossible for the analysand to take his internal movements seriously knowing that his analyst is sitting there tranquilly, smoking his cigarette and reacting, at most, with the stereotyped question: "Now what comes into your mind about that?" (1931/1994o, p. 129).

The idea that the psychoanalyst is called upon by the intricacies of the clinical environment to adopt a sensitive presence leads Ferenczi (1928/1994l) to research the "metapsychology of the analyst's mental processes during analysis" which, as the session goes on, oscillates between empathic identification, on the one hand, and intellectual self-control and activity on the other. A passage from "The Elasticity of the Psychoanalytic Technique" is quite enlightening on the complexity of the psychoanalyst's work:

> *He has to let the patient's free associations play upon him; simultaneously he lets his own fantasy get to work with the association material; from time to time he compares the new connections that arise with earlier results of the analysis; and not for one moment must he relax the vigilance and criticism made necessary by his own subjective trends (Ferenczi, 1928/1994l, p. 96)*

Ferenczi concludes his presentation of the empathic style in psychoanalysis by indicating that the "strain" to which the analyst is exposed would call for the profession to reflect on a "special hygiene for the analyst" — which we are referring to as the analyst's *health*. As a matter of fact, termination of analysis, by providing the "unhampered mobility of the libido" and the possibility of a "free enjoyment of life" would be the privileged access route to the analyst's health and hygiene; for Ferenczi (1928/1994l, p. 99), health will be synonymous with *elasticity*.

In "The Problem of the Termination of the Analysis", Ferenczi reiterates his conviction that there is "no difference between a therapeutic and a training analysis". The distinction comes from the fact that the patient can interrupt his analysis at will, while the analyst in training needs to complete the process, with a "complete ending of the analysis" (1927/1994j, p. 84). However, before pointing out some questions raised by Ferenczi regarding the termination of the analysis, it is worth underlining the historical importance of this essay, based on his lecture presented at the 10th International Psychoanalytical Congress, in Innsbruck. As far as my research has discovered, it is the first psychoanalytic text dedicated to the termination of the analysis. Freud's 1937/1964b essay, translated as "Analysis Terminable and

Interminable", is largely a response to Ferenczi's writing and some of his criticisms relating to his brief analysis with Freud. In the 1950s and 1960s, Jacques Lacan took up several of Ferenczi's arguments in his pivotal reflections about the termination of analyses and the process of psychoanalytic training (*cf.* Bernardes, 2002).

Two points made by Ferenczi in his essay are worth mentioning: first, the unequivocal perception that the termination of the analysis entails a deep and comprehensive mourning work by the analysand, through which he can dispense with the satisfactions provided by the analytic situation itself. To that end, though, the psychoanalyst must bear his dismissal delicately and, above all, quite patiently, as already indicated, keeping his narcissism under strict control. Furthermore, in an implicit reference to his relationship with Freud, Ferenczi touches on an extremely controversial topic. Let us be literal: "Every male patient must attain a feeling of equality in relation to the physician as a sign that he has overcome his fear of castration; every female patient [...] must have got rid of her masculinity complex [...]" (1927/1994j, p. 84).

In "Analysis Terminable and Interminable", Freud (1937/1964b, p. 250–253) refers to this passage, declaring that "Ferenczi was asking a very great deal". In fact, in the last chapter of his essay Freud had formulated the "bedrock of castration", understood as the "repudiation of femininity", as the last degree of resistance to psychoanalysis. We read in Freud:

> *At no other point in one's analytic work does one suffer more from an oppressive feeling that [...] one has been "preaching to the winds", than when one is trying to persuade a woman to abandon her wish for a penis [...] or when one is seeking to convince a man that* a passive attitude to men does not always signify castration and that it is indispensable in many relationships in life. *The rebellious overcompensation of the male produces one of*

> *the strongest transference-resistances. He refuses to subject himself to a father-substitute, or to feel indebted to him for anything, and consequently he refuses to accept his recovery from the doctor. (Freud, 1937/1964b, p. 250–253)*

We are apparently facing a dialogue of the deaf (perhaps it is the "obtuseness of the analyst" mentioned by Ferenczi). After all, Freud too believes it is not just a clash over the theory of the clinic; the specter of Ferenczi's criticisms surrounds his considerations. Thus, on the one hand, Freud responds to Ferenczi's judgment in the famous letter of January 17, 1930 (presented in Chapter 1) that he (Freud) had not allowed the analysis of Ferenczi's negative transference, keeping himself in the place of "adored master" and "unattainable ideal", stating that not every good relationship between analyst and analysand would be of a transference nature, there being also "friendly relations which were based on reality and which proved to be viable" (Freud, 1937/1964b, p. 222). There is a clear similarity in the construction of the Freudian argument referring to the termination of the analysis, where he claims that a man's passive attitude towards others "does not always signify castration and that it is indispensable in many relationships in life".

However, the argument highlighted by Ferenczi at various points in his clinical trajectory is that the analyst needs to authorize the expression of the analysand's hostile movements in transference, indicative of the work of detachment of the object that had been incorporated by the traumatic disavowal. Otherwise, it would be necessary for the psychoanalyst to allow himself to be deprived of his responsibility — and to be destroyed — for each analysis to come to an end (Robert, 2015). Nevertheless, psychoanalysts often resist the destructive gesture of their analysands through an affective detachment that denotes more than a technical orthodoxy, but a true *resistance to the clinical encounter*. According to Ferenczi, it would be necessary for the psychoanalyst to sustain a *resistance within the encounter* with the affects manifested by the analysand. The psychoanalyst's resistance *within* the analytic encounter is a condition for the experience of recognition required for the working-through of the analysand's core traumatic contents and for the mourning work that leads to the termination of the analysis.

In training analyses, Ferenczi's analysis with Freud being a paradigmatic example, the problem worsens since the psychoanalyst often occupies the position of a master in an institutional context shared with his analysand. Freud was not only the creator of psychoanalysis — having chosen Ferenczi as his favorite disciple — but was also Ferenczi's analyst and close friend. In this specific case (noting that training analyses tend to reproduce this structure of "master and pupil", perpetuating dependence), Ferenczi's preservation of a "passive stance" was rather convenient for the harmony of the psychoanalytic movement, and his submission to a "father substitute" was quite desirable for Freud *(cf.* Kupermann, 2014b, Chapter 5).

For Ferenczi, there would be nothing more harmful to the course of treatment than the "schoolmasterish, or even an authoritative, attitude on the physician's part". In his opinion, the "empathy rule"[15] was opposed to the "lofty attitude to the patient generally adopted by the omniscient and omnipotent doctor". The psychoanalyst's "modesty", he argued, would be nothing more than "a reflection of the limitations of our knowledge" (1928/1994l, p. 94). On the other hand, the analyst's claims to omniscience and omnipotence are considered to be defenses against the fear of madness — a fear, caused by the experience of radical helplessness, that is the last bastion of resistance to the analytic experience (Ferenczi, 1932/1988).

The *Clinical Diary* entry from March 13, 1932 is entitled "A two-children analysis". In it, Ferenczi reaches the culmination point of the thesis presented in "Child-Analysis in the Analysis of Adults"

15 Translated from the German word *Einfühlungsregel* (Ferenczi, 1928/1939, p. 390).

(1931/19940), according to which analysis is only successful insofar as it manages to touch the child, often seriously split, in the patient.[16] With the turning point of 1928, his clinical experience had indicated that in order to have access to the child in the analysand, the psychoanalyst would need to access his own child — which is, presumably, one of the goals, in the Ferenczian notion, of the termination of analysis. The passage is precious:

> *Certain phases of mutual analysis represent the complete renunciation of all compulsion and of all authority on both sides: they give the impression of* two *equally terrified* children *who compare their experiences, and because of their common fate understand each other completely and instinctively try to comfort each other. Awareness of this* shared fate *allows the partner to appear as completely harmless, therefore as someone whom one can trust with confidence. [...] children unite among themselves and form alliances of friendship. (Should the analysis terminate under the signs of such a friendship?) (Ferenczi, 1932/1988, p. 56)*

The transcript above ends with a question mark that will lead us to the last chapter of the book, on the objectives of analysis according to Ferenczi. However, we must point out that this passage also offers a solution, quite different from that given by Freud, to the problem of friendship between analyst and analysand. It is known that Freud did not have access to the *Clinical Diary*, which was kept by Michael Balint for years, waiting for an opportunity to be published, coming to light only in 1985 in France, fifty-three years after it was written.

Freud believed friendship would be synonymous with the recognition of the authority of a father substitute, while Ferenczi

16 It should be noted that this also applies to the treatment of children, especially those who, due to their clinical condition, are unable to play.

thought friendship would be closer to the establishment of a horizontal relationship characterized by the refusal of masochistic servitude,[17] a sign of the mutual freedom experienced by those with a shared fate (*cf.* Prado de Oliveira, 2012). Friendship would therefore be characteristic of the condition of being an orphan — the position in which the subject finds himself at the end of the analysis.

4.6 *The condition of being an orphan*

Some commentators and even detractors of Ferenczi (and other authors representing object relation theories in psychoanalysis) associate his concept of clinical practice with an exercise in which the psychoanalyst would occupy a maternal position that would, at its limit, tend to keep analysands dependent on the analyst.[18] On the other hand, the Freudian path showed how clinical practice governed by the principle of abstinence in the transference field, which aims for the assumption of castration by the analysand, entails a paternal position on the part of the analyst (Freud, 1937/1964b). Nevertheless, the various roadblocks encountered by Freud revealed that in acting as a "father substitute", the analyst tends to reinforce the masochism of analysands, who will tolerate the greatest types of violence imposed — mostly inadvertently, of course — by their own analysts. The Wolf Man case study, as we have seen, abundantly illustrates the iatrogenic failure of the "paternal" style in psychoanalysis.

For Ferenczi, however, if the technique inspired by the interpretive style was able, effectively, to become "sadistic", on the other hand, an attempt at a "mothering" approach would risk being "hypocritical". This is because the greatest resistance to analysis, in this argument,

17 I refer the reader once again to the concept of friendship proposed by Marilena Chaui (1987), which is very much in tune with Ferenczi's proposal.

18 Interestingly, neither Ferenczi nor Winnicott, the two main targets of this criticism, had children.

results from the insensitivity of the analyst, i.e., from his denial of the ways in which he is affected by the clinical encounter. In the last year of his life, through "mutual analysis", Ferenczi (1932/1988) sought to rid the analytical space of all defensive hypocrisy, calling on the psychoanalyst to recognize and face the traumatisms resulting from his clinical practice. This took him to the conclusion that the analytical encounter often conjured up an image of two children who, equally helpless, establish a *shared fate* to achieve the experience of tenderness necessary for the advent of their creative authenticity.

5. Neocatharsis and the sensitive way of working-through

The sudden emergence in modern psycho-analysis of portions of an earlier technique and theory should not dismay us; it merely reminds us that, so far, no single advance has been made in analysis which has had to be entirely discarded as useless, and that we must constantly be prepared to find new veins of gold in temporarily abandoned workings.

(Ferenczi, 1930/1994n, p. 120)

Although there is no specific work by Ferenczi on the goals of psychoanalytic treatment, it can be said that his interest in the issue of the termination of analysis — which was a pioneering inquiry, in the context of the history of psychoanalysis — gives us some valuable clues about his conceptions on the topic.

Effectively, in "The Problem of the Termination of the Analysis", Ferenczi (1927/1994j) outlines some of the criteria for considering an analysis completed. The context in which this essay comes to light is, as previously demonstrated, revealing: not only because it is the first work dedicated to the subject, which predates by nine years Freud's "Analysis Terminable and Interminable" (1937/1964b), but also because Ferenczi's interest in the terminability of analysis coincides with his concern about the competences that should be developed by the analyst so that he can accurately exercise his office. His formulation of a desirable elasticity of technique (Ferenczi, 1928/1994l) required from the psychoanalyst an unprecedented sensitive availability, for the treatment to be able to achieve its goals.

Consequently, thinking about the termination of an analysis in the context of its aim and purpose also entailed postulating that a psychoanalyst is, with priority over any other "patient", the one who should have conducted his analysis to a conclusion. This led him to propose that the analyst's own analysis should be the "second fundamental rule" of psychoanalysis. In other words, in order for the analyst to achieve, together with the analysands, the expected goals of the treatment, it was necessary that the psychoanalyst himself had overcome the main obstacles encountered in the course of his own analysis.

A few years later, in the first entry of his *Clinical Diary,* Ferenczi (1932/1988) would point to the "hypocrisy of analysts" as the most powerful source of resistance to analysis. In other words (he argued), the psychoanalyst's refusal to admit his affects in the context of clinical practice — his "hypocrisy" — would itself produce the greatest resistance to the actual work of analysis on the patient.

These introductory considerations allow us to return to the problem of the "lie" and its relation to the privileged objectives of an analysis.

5.1 The school of authenticity: from repression to splitting

Based on the comments on a case in which the analysand's symptom consisted of a "need" to lie, Ferenczi explicitly suggests that one of the main goals of psychoanalytic treatment is to overcome lying. It reads: "A real abandonment of mendacity therefore appears to be at least a sign of the approaching end of the analysis" (1927/1994j, p. 78).

Jacques Lacan, the main heir of the Ferenczian discussion about "The Problem of the Termination of the Analysis" (*cf.* Izcovith, 2009; *cf.* Tardits, 2009), contributes by reinforcing the argument that the issue of lying is central — as is its opposite, authenticity — in his last contributions to the theory of the clinic when referring to "Ferenczi's school of authenticity" (Lacan, 1955/2006a, p. 288). I believe that it is above all from his interaction with the first paragraphs of Ferenczi's essay about the relationship between mendacity and termination of analysis that Lacan finds and raises the issue of authenticity, on the part both of the analysand and the analyst.[1] Let us try to understand, then, what the psychical recourse to lying means for Ferenczi.

A more orthodox metapsychological reading, such as the one proposed by Alexandre Stevens (1992), would understand the "lie" to which Ferenczi refers to be the effect of the phantom in the constitution of the repressed. In this case, the purpose of analysis would be to unveil the subjective position taken, as a defense against the state of helplessness, by the analysand in relation to the Other. It is indeed possible to find good indications in the Ferenczian text to support this understanding. Ferenczi wrote (1927/1994j, p. 79): "What in the light of morality and of the reality principle we call a lie, in the case of an infant and in terms of pathology we call a fantasy". However, the clinical matrix on which Stevens bases his reading of lying is that of the repressed, in which the treatment of neuroses, with emphasis on hysteria, is the horizon of the psychoanalytic clinic. After all, if we go back to the 19th century, we will remember that the main reason for Freud to abandon the theory of traumatic seduction was the formulation of the concept of fantasy, primarily inspired by the hysteric's "first lie" (*proton pseudos*). In other words, the scenes reported by the patients said less about any memory concerning factual reality than about their Oedipal desires (*cf.* Freud, 1950[1895]/1966b; 1897/1966a).

---

1 For a deeper understanding of the problem of authenticity in the works of Ferenczi and Lacan, I refer the reader to Daniel Migliani Vitorello (2015).

On the other hand, a closer look at the issues Ferenczi was delving into when "The Problem of the Termination of the Analysis" was published brings us to new landscapes in the area of psychopathology and clinical theory: the return to the issue of trauma and its effects on subjectivity, illustrated by the suffering observed in patients treated by Ferenczi. In this context, the reference for the "lie" would no longer be repression, but what Ferenczi, in the final period of his work, called "splitting".

The clinical case reported in "The Problem of the Termination of the Analysis" evokes two different situations, both referring to the theme of lying. The first one refers to the fact that the analysand had been, for many months, "deceiving me the whole time in connection with an important circumstance of a financial nature" (Ferenczi, 1927/1994j, p. 77). The second one refers to a session the patient failed to appear for and denied doing so in the following session, "obstinately" insisting that he had attended the session in which he was effectively absent (Ferenczi, 1927/1994j, p. 77). The analysis went on to reveal a kind of amnesia regarding all events of that day, caused by a state of intoxication, a situation that had already occurred at other times in the patient's life. These two events are paradigmatic for the proposed discussion. It is worth citing Ferenczi's comment: "When I obtained incontrovertible evidence of his conscious mendacity I was convinced that the *split personality, at any rate in his case*, was only the neurotic sign of his mendacity, a kind of indirect confession of his character-defect (Ferenczi, 1927/1994j, p. 78).

However, what would be irreducible to this analysand is extended to all subjects who are victims of splitting. In a footnote added to the same paragraph we read:

> *I have no hesitation in generalizing this single observation, and interpreting all cases of so-called split personality as symptoms of partially conscious insincerity which force those liable to it to manifest in turn only parts of their*

> *personality. In terms of metapsychology, one might say that these people have several super-egos which they have failed to fuse. (Ferenczi, 1927/1994j, p. 78)*

It is understood that "these people" to which Ferenczi refers, who present the symptom of insincerity, are precisely the patients who forced him to return to the issue of traumatogenesis in the late 1920s.

5.2 Encountering the traumatic

To briefly recapitulate our journey, we saw how Ferenczi's goal in using the active technique (1919–1926) was precisely to encourage stagnant treatments to reach termination. The use of prohibitions and injunctions was aimed at barring, in the name of the principle of abstinence, any substitute instinctual satisfaction experienced in the transference field by promoting frustration, the emergence of hostile affects (negative transference) aimed at the analyst, and associative work (*cf.* Ferenczi, 1919/1994e). The culmination of this clinical style can be found in "On Forced Phantasies (Activity in the Association Technique)" (Ferenczi, 1924/1994h).

In this essay, Ferenczi exposes a case that presented management difficulties very close to those reported by Freud with the Wolf Man (which we discussed in Chapter 2). It was an analysand who, despite being friendly towards the analyst, did not make any progress in his analysis. A first gesture toward overcoming the analysand's resistances was inspired by the unorthodox device employed by Freud: Ferenczi also established a deadline for the completion of his patient's treatment. The effect was null, and the analysand, paralyzed in his associative flow, nevertheless insisted on being friendly and grateful. Dissatisfied, Ferenczi began to act to arouse aggressive fantasies directed at the analyst, which culminated in the analysand's evocation of a sadomasochistic sexual scene.

In the scene evoked by Ferenczi's account, the analysand sexually possessed his analyst. But what at first could resemble a sadistic fantasy — an expression of the hostility that stemmed from the Oedipus complex — was actually a *masochistic* donation of the analysand; his *obedient* response to the intrusive demands promoted by the "active" analyst. Just as, once the deadline for the end of the treatment was established, Serguéi offered Freud the dream of the wolves, which gave him the key to access the traumatic primary scene and to the construction of the history of his infantile neurosis.

According to Freud (1918[1914]/1955b) in a controversial formulation regarding the case, the repressed material emerged with a clarity akin to that obtained with hypnosis; Freud had abandoned the hypnotic technique decades earlier, mainly due to his perception that hypnosis, by not recognizing the value of patients' resistance, put them in a transference position of dependence and submission that was difficult to dissolve.

We have already sufficiently demonstrated how disastrous the outcome of the treatment was: Serguéi had become seriously ill and, after World War II, returned to Vienna to treat the remainder of his transference with Freud. Ruth Brunswick (see Chapter 1) did not fail to make an accurate critique of the technical procedure used by Freud: the fact that the psychoanalyst has obtained the biographical facts that allow him to construct the history of the patient's neurosis does not mean that the treatment is completed. It would still be necessary to "know to what extent the patient needs to 'rework' (*Durcharbeiten*) his material to be able to cure himself" (Brunswick, 1928/1981, p. 309). After all, according to what was revealed in this second analysis, the Wolf Man had not managed to get rid of the "fear of an autonomous existence" and of his "fixation to his father" (Brunswick, 1928/1981, p. 309).

In noticing the irreducible tendency of some analysands to maintain themselves in an object position in relation to the demands of their "significant others", Ferenczi came up against the traumatic, which led him to review the use of the active technique. As Freud once said, "the lion only springs once",[2] and the shot had backfired. In other words, the attempt to carry stagnant analyses to completion by threatening the analysands with abandonment ended up causing an increase in their adherence to the idealized persecutory objects.

5.3 Trauma and its enclosure: who is lying?

Listening to the so-called "difficult patients" led Ferenczi to formulate a trauma theory based on the notions of disavowal (*Verleugnung*), identification with the aggressor, and traumatic progression. The central reasoning of his argument lies in the attempt to explain the identifying consequences of a traumatic experience.

As previously explained, what characterized trauma for Ferenczi was less the experience of the aggression suffered, which we call the first time of trauma, and more the *disavowal* inflicted by the second trusted person, other than the aggressor, who was sought to witness the analysand's pain and attribute meaning to the violation. In the case of the child, this second person is another adult he turns to; in the case of an adult who has had their integrity violated, this second person would be an equal, or even care institutions. Since the notion of "disavowal" plays a leading role in our argument, it is appropriate to return to the times of Ferenczi's traumatogenesis, stressing that Ferenczi built his theory on the understanding that the unbearable suffering of his analysands was the effect of traumatic events — especially those that resulted in static and mimetic identifications with persecutory objects.

Ergo, the starting point of all psychic suffering would be the intense love bond between a child and an adult, broken in a brutal and

2 In reference to the active technique, Freud (1937/1964b, p. 219) had written: "A miscalculation cannot be rectified. The saying that a lion only springs once must apply here".

indecipherable way by the violation suffered. Aggression on the part of the adult would thus characterize the first moment of the traumatic event, incomprehensible to the child who, unable to name his pain, would be thrown into what we call the *time of the unspeakable*.

Since the tendency of psychical movement is *introjection* to constitute the senses through which the subject recognizes himself as the creator of objects worthy of his loving investment, the abused child will seek another adult, different from the aggressor, with whom he established a relationship of trust to be the recipient of his nameless suffering, to help him symbolize it (*cf.* Balint, 1969). As mentioned previously (see Chapter 3), I call this second moment of the traumatic event the *time of testimony*; we will also look at how transference-regression in the psychoanalytic treatment seeks to reestablish the experience of testimony in conditions that are favorable to the production of meanings by the analysand.

The traumatic event itself is established in a third moment, characterized by the failure of the victim's testimony, in which his voice could not be heard and the construction of his version of the traumatic event could not be recognized: the *time of disavowal*. By stating that "the worst way of dealing with such situations is that of *disavowal* [*Verleugnung*] of their existence", Ferenczi (1931/19940, p. 138) makes explicit the concept that it is the enclosure of the labyrinth of lying that effectively provokes the experience of trauma.

In that sense, trauma would be the effect of a lie by the adult who was resorted to in the name of trust (and also of the aggressor himself, as we will see) built through the hypocritical "disavowal" of the ever-hesitant and vulnerable version of the traumatized child or subject. But who is it that lies in the vicious circle of traumatism, and to whom?

Since, as we have seen, the aggressor is always a loved one, in the sense of the so-called "language of tenderness" — someone the child effectively *depends* upon to face his helplessness — for such children the defensive solution, so as not to see themselves as being fully abandoned, is to fully "identify themselves with the aggressor" (Ferenczi, 1933/1994q, p. 162). Without finding resonance for his testimony, the child's only option is to give in to the *lie* of the one who violated him. "Almost always", writes Ferenczi, "the perpetrator behaves as though nothing had happened", a lie that tends to impose itself on both parties to the traumatic experience, either out of guilt, shame, or fear of punishment. In this way, the aggressor lies to himself and to the violated child because he cannot bear the burden of his own accountability, and the traumatized subject "lies", because he cannot tolerate the loneliness engendered by the abandonment he was subjected to (Ferenczi, 1933/1994q, p. 163).

In the victim, unable to express his indignation and hatred, the identification with the aggressor, together with the "incorporation" of his guilt, reveals the strategy adopted by the subject to survive the death agony caused by the injustice suffered and by the unrepresentable dimension of the traumatic excess. In this case, the *inability* to be alone[3] is irreducible, and it is not possible to express any ambivalence in relation to the object with whom he has identified.

Identification with the aggressor, in turn, promotes a narcissistic splitting of the self in his traumatized subjectivity. Without having someone close who can take care of him, the subject, now split into a destroyed sensitive part and an omniscient but numb part, begins to play the role of his own mother or father, making the abandonment null and void.

The metaphor used by Ferenczi (1933/1994q) to illustrate the subjective condition of the traumatized subject is that of the fruit which, contaminated by a bird or insect, becomes ripe on the outside, while it has been destroyed on the inside. In this sense, one can follow his formulation of a traumatic progression through which the

3 In the last pages of the *Clinical Diary*, Ferenczi explains the issue of traumatic isolation: "BEING ALONE leads to splitting" (1932/1988, p. 201, capital letters in original).

subject matures too quickly, adapting to the intrusive environment by submissively identifying with the aggressor, paying the price for what we can recognize as a loss of his *authenticity*. The incorporated object effectively remains as a foreign body, a modality of non-integrated tyrannical superego, a true phantom to which the subject subordinates himself in a masochistic fashion. As Ferenczi (1932/1988) writes in his *Clinical Diary*, masochism always entails the search for pain as the alleviation of greater pains.

However, also in the *Diary*, we find a significant passage that offers an attempt to answer the question of the fate of the core of the sensitive dimension split off the ego. In the entry of January 24, 1932, we read:

> *The content of the split-off ego is always as follows: natural development and spontaneity, protest against violence and injustice, contemptuous, perhaps sarcastic and ironic obedience displayed in the face of domination, but inward knowledge that the violence has in fact achieved nothing; it has altered only something objective, the decision-making process, but not the ego as such. (Ferenczi, 1932/1988, p. 19)*

5.4 Neocatharsis, construction, and "becoming-child"

In "The Principle of Relaxation and Neocatharsis", Ferenczi illustrates with a case study the clinical style he developed for the treatment of traumatized patients who have incorporated the object that persecuted them. The patient, after a few years of manifestations of negative transference due to what Ferenczi called a "hard struggle with resistance", says to her analyst: "Now I like you and now I can let you go" (Ferenczi, 1930/1994n, p. 123). He concludes that the analysand's embarrassment because of her hatred towards the object she could not get rid of, directed towards the analyst in transference, is more restrictive than the embarrassment produced by any love bond. In fact, for Ferenczi, the driving force of all irremovable adhesiveness of the transference is the hate that has not been able to gain expression. We read: "Repressed hate often operates more strongly in the direction of fixation and arrest than openly confessed tenderness" (Ferenczi, 1930/1994n, p. 123).

This reveals that the elasticity of the technique, formulated for handling "difficult" cases, entailed the unequivocal acceptance of repetition in analysis, with an emphasis on the management of negative transference — noting that the latter was always the subject of great reservation by Freud (*cf.* Robert & Kupermann, 2012; 2015). There is a famous passage in which Ferenczi creates an analogy between the psychoanalyst and the "Aunt Sally" — a target on whom the patient can exercise his affects of resentment and hostility. Ferenczi (1928/1994l, p. 93) adds: "If we do not protect ourselves from this, but, on the contrary, encourage the only-too-hesitant patient at every opportunity that presents itself, sooner or later we shall reap the well-deserved reward of our patience in the form of the arrival of the positive transference".

The discrepancy between the "patience" proposed by Ferenczi and the active technique employed by Freud in treating the Wolf Man, and by Ferenczi himself in the case reported in "On Forced Phantasies", is plainly evident (see Chapter 2). It is precisely this contrast that supports our hypothesis that the Ferenczian clinical style, developed after the turning point of 1928 and characterized by the sign of neocatharsis, is heir to the impasses imposed on the psychoanalytic technique by the borderline cases mentioned by Freud in "Remembering, Repeating, and Working-Through" (1914/1958c).

In fact, in "The Problem of the Termination of the Analysis", Ferenczi differentiates a *qualitative* aspect of analysis — aimed at the topical-dynamic elucidation of the repressed matter and of symptom formation, promoted by interpretation — from a *quantitative* one, referring to the economic element of the psychic apparatus, which requires working-through. Ferenczi writes:

> *In the course of the time at our disposal, not only must the whole unconscious psychical material be lived through again in the form of memories and repetitions, but the third factor in analytic technique must also be applied. I refer to the factor of analytic working through. Freud has emphasized that this factor is as important as the other two, but its importance has not been properly appreciated. (Ferenczi, 1927/1994j, p. 82)*

The clinical style created by Ferenczi aimed to broaden the applicability of psychoanalytic treatment to non-neurotic conditions, which required Freud to pay greater attention to working-through and to prevent the repetition of iatrogenic situations such as the one experienced by him and the Wolf Man. In close harmony with Ruth Brunswick's observations, Ferenczi had emphasized the importance of working-through by stating that "This [qualitative analysis] can be nearly complete without producing the expected therapeutic change" (Ferenczi, 1927/1994j, p. 82).

Going back to Freud's essay (1914/1958c), we saw how working-through requires the *time* for the patient to experience his resistances, which is a "trial of patience" for the psychoanalyst — while on the other hand, it is also the most transformative aspect of the psychoanalytic treatment, which unequivocally differentiates it from suggestion and investigative hypnosis. In theoretical terms, Freud (1914/1958c, p. 156) compared the working-through to the "'abreacting' of the quotas of affect strangulated by repression — an abreaction without which hypnotic treatment remained ineffective".

Freud's allusion to the cathartic method practiced in the 19th century, precisely in a period marked by the wide diffusion of psychoanalysis and the improvement of the psychoanalytic technique, is indeed surprising. As indicated, the reference to cathartic abreaction was intended, on the one hand, to *repair* the damage caused by the use of the "active" device in Serguéi Pankejeff's analysis, which ended in that same summer of 1914. Furthermore, with his reflections on working-through, Freud demonstrated the need to bring back the notion that, during the course of treatment, the psychoanalyst also *works* "in common with his patient" (Freud, 1914/1958c, p. 155).

The notion of the psychoanalyst's "work" appears at crucial moments in Freud's theory of the technique. A first reference can be found in "The Psychotherapy of Hysteria", the first essay on clinical psychology *per se*, in which Freud (1893–1895/1955a, p. 270) indicates that overcoming the analysand's resistances requires "psychical work" by the psychoanalyst. After taking up the question again in "Remembering, Repeating, and Working-Through", Freud expands on the issue in "Constructions in Analysis" (1937/1964c), an essay written a few years after Ferenczi's death, dedicating himself to reflecting on what he calls the psychoanalyst's "task", "endeavor", and, finally, "work" of construction or reconstruction.

His starting point is that analysis, on the one hand, summons the analysand to "recollect" his repressed past. It would be necessary, though, to remember a "fundamental fact" that seems so obvious it has been relegated to the background: the fact that "the work of analysis consists of two quite different portions, that it is carried on in two separate localities, that it involves two people, to each of whom a distinct task is assigned" (Freud, 1937/1964c, p. 258). *No other passage in Freud's work so categorically states that clinical work entails an intersubjective encounter*, for which the psychoanalyst's sensitive availability to affect and let himself be affected by the analysand is an absolutely necessary condition. Freud also emphasizes that sensitivity is essential to know "the time and manner, [...] as well as the explanations" with which the analyst will be able to convey his constructions, thus establishing "the link between the two portions of the work of analysis", his and the analysand's.

The notion of "construction" postulated by Freud points, on the one hand, to the limits of interpretation — defined as partial — since it refers to a single element indicating the return of the repressed, such as a dream fragment or a slip of the tongue. On the other hand, it points to the limits of the field of representation, meaning that not everything can be recalled by the analysand. However, that which is not remembered is acted out, primarily through the repetitions that appear in the transference field.

Consequently, the work of the analyst would be akin to the archaeologist's, who recreates ancient buildings and objects by inference, from the remains that have survived the effect of time. And yet, the conditions are more favorable, since the "psychical object" is somehow preserved. According to Freud, "even things that seem completely forgotten are present somehow and somewhere, and have merely been buried and made inaccessible to the subject" (Freud, 1937/1964c, p. 260).

But since what is accessible in these cases is not the intact memory, the psychoanalyst is forced to resort to his own imagination so that, from the fragments presented and brought to light, and the previously known material about the patient's history, he can convey his construction to the analysand. Freud (1937/1964c, p. 268–269) goes so far as to indicate a proximity between the construction work and "delusions" typically seen in hallucination, stating that delusion opens up a path of access to "historical truth". Lizana Dallazen (2017), seeking to clarify this clinical problem, proposed that it would be up to the analyst to *work through* the countertransference — with emphasis on the hallucinatory elements caused by it — so as to transform the fragments acted out by the analysand into constructions of his history, able to make possible the conviction that is necessary for him to give meaning to his suffering.

Published in the same year as "Analysis Terminable and Interminable" (1937/1964b), "Constructions in Analysis" confirms Ferenczi's evident posthumous influence on Freud's final clinical essays. If, in the former, Freud rebuts Ferenczi's reproaches to his performance as an analyst and criticizes his disciple's considerations about the termination of analysis, in the latter he makes a theoretical effort to include Ferenczi's formulations on neocatharsis into his clinical theory. In fact, Ferenczi had postulated years before that neocatharsis is the way through which the analyst has access to the parts that were split off by the traumatic event, thus making possible his work of *constructing* the analysand's "historical truth".

It would not be an exaggeration to say, therefore, that at the origin of Freud's formulation of "constructions" in analysis is Ferenczi's attempt to improve the psychoanalytic method for the treatment of analysands who are entangled by their attempts to gain testimony for the traumatic unrepresentable.

***

Ferenczi returns to the problem of working-through in "The Principle of Relaxation and Neocatharsis" to, in his own words, "restore in the relation between analyst and patient the affectivity which, as was now plain, had for a time been unduly neglected" (1930/1994n, p. 110). In his assessment, "the highly emotional relation between physician and patient, which resembled that in hypnotic suggestion", which had marked the dawn of the psychoanalytic experience, had progressively cooled down to the point of becoming an "unending association-experiment" characteristic of a "mainly intellectual" process (Ferenczi, 1930/1994n, p. 110).

The principle of relaxation, also named by Ferenczi as *Prinzip der Gewährung* (something like the *principle of consent*),[4] opposed the

4 In the French edition, *Prinzip der Gewährung* was translated as *principle of laisser-faire.*

principle of abstinence in its economic sense (not ethical, it should be noted),[5] since it aimed to maintain the frustration-drive in the analytic setting, according to the understanding that only under psychic tension would the analysand "work". Ferenczi (1930/1994n, p. 110) nevertheless revives the assumption that in the fundamental rule of psychoanalysis, *free association*, there is an invitation to "freedom of speech and expression of [...] feelings", without which the psychoanalytic method would become unrecognizable.

Thus, in every analytical process — Ferenczi's argument continues — there would be a competition between the principle of abstinence and the principle of relaxation: an excessively rigid analyst would tend to cause a superfluous increase in the analysand's resistances, promoting "a too literal repetition of traumatic incidents in the patient's childhood". In this sense, he confesses: "In the course of my practical analytical work, which extended over many years, I constantly found myself infringing one or another of Freud's injunctions in his 'Recommendations on Technique'" (Ferenczi, 1930/1994n, p. 114).

The freedom created by the principle of relaxation made the setting more "elastic", giving rise to an affective closeness between analyst and analysand and creating what Ferenczi called an "atmosphere of confidence" (Ferenczi, 1930/1994n, p. 118). And only the establishment of the lost *confidence* would allow the emergence of the *time of testimony* in the analytical situation, preventing the traumatic *disavowal* from being repeated in the course of the analysis. In fact, if in the description of traumatogenesis, the loss of confidence in loved ones culminates in the identification with the aggressor and in taking refuge in splitting, it is the restoration of the bond of confidence with the analyst that makes the clinical gesture effective.

5 The ethical meaning of the principle of abstinence is the inescapable imperative that the analyst is not authorized to make the analysand the object of his own jouissance.

This clinical stance also favored, as would be expected, the emergence of negative transference and the expression of aggressiveness and destructiveness towards the analyst. Ferenczi's intuition that only the unimpeded exercise of ambivalence could free the analysand from the tyranny of identification with the aggressor thus gained methodological consistency. In his words, "Finally, I was able to state that not only did my patients' analysis not suffer from the greater freedom accorded them, but, after all their aggressive impulses had exhausted their fury, positive transference and also much more positive results were achieved" (Ferenczi, 1930/1994n, p. 113).

The surprise, however, was the manifestation of hysterical bodily symptoms, and even "trances" in which the repetition gained a clear individual character, giving access to the "dissociated parts" in the analysand. Ferenczi (1930/1994n, p. 119) interpreted these movements as signs of regression to the stages in which the analysand had experienced traumatic events that were hitherto intangible, which, in this way, were expressed through physical memories. The unrepresentable, as it could not be signified in words, was presented through physical materializations and exhibitions of repetition fragments acted out by the analysand. The reach of the traumatic memory material thus acquired, through "reconstructions" in the analysis, an unprecedented "feeling of reality and concreteness" (*Dinghaftigkeit*), which brought the clinical material closer to the "phenomena of the Breuer-Freud catharsis" (Ferenczi, 1930/1994n, p. 119).

Consequently, it appears as though neocatharsis, as presented to the psychoanalytic community by Ferenczi, stems from the clinical style adopted since the turning point of 1928, illustrated by the principle of relaxation. Furthermore, it seems that its characteristic elements are *regression* in the context of transference — allowing access to the analysand's split nuclei which, in turn, inspire analytical constructions — and the *game* of shared affects that allow, firstly, the exercise of the ambivalence required to free the analysand from his identification with the incorporated object, and secondly, the experience of primordial omnipotence capable of awakening vital impulses and the desire to continue to exist. In sum, regression (*thalassal* regression, as we will see later in the text) and game are the pillars of the neocatharsis postulated by Ferenczi to address the suffering of the analysands with split personalities that he welcomed to his couch.

However, Ferenczi states that there is an irreducible difference between neocatharsis and the "fragmentary eruptions of emotion and recollection which the primitive catharsis could provoke and which had only a temporary effect". Further on, we read:

> *The catharsis of which I am speaking is, like many dreams, only a confirmation from the unconscious, a sign that our toilsome* analytical construction, *our technique of dealing with resistance and transference, have finally succeeded in drawing near to the aetiological reality. There is little that the paleocatharsis has in common with this* neocatharsis. *(Ferenczi, 1930/1994n, p. 119)*

If we can effectively consider neocatharsis as the culmination of Ferenczi's theoretical-clinical contributions, it is because by formulating it he summed up the answer to the challenge of working through affects in the clinic — faithful to Freud's statement that his inspiration resided in the *cathartic abreaction* presented in *Studies on Hysteria* (Breuer & Freud, 1893–1895/1955) — with the necessary reference to the role of the traumatic disavowal imposed on the subject when seeking testimony for his pain.

As such, in referring to the quantitative aspect of the clinical exercise and the work of affects carried out by the patient with the analyst's participation, Ferenczi's neocatharsis brought the psychoanalytic experience closer to a space of play and affective sharing, similar to the clinical practice with children, an innovation of the psychoanalytic field in the 1920s. For this reason, every analysis would effectively be an analysis of the child who inhabits each analysand.

On one occasion, Anna Freud told Ferenczi: "You treat your patients as I treat the children whom I analyse". Ferenczi agreed, noting that his practice of measures for relaxation "assuredly obliterates even more completely the distinction between the analysis of children and that of adults" (1930/1994n, p. 122).

Thus, on the horizon of psychoanalytic treatment lies the attribute of "becoming-child", in the sense proposed by Chaim Katz (1996, p. 90–94):

> *the fact and act of becoming [... which is...] a product of encounters and chance. There is no predetermined path that the child should follow in order to become an adult. Thus, being a child is not just about obeying the powers, but an immanent exercise of powers [...] carried out in new encounters and incessantly sought in intensities.*

Indeed, bringing the language of infantile tenderness back to life, as advocated by Ferenczi, means enabling the subject to regain the intensity of the word that evokes the self and reality, ensuring a more authentic existence. "And a child", continues Katz, "expressively says what he thinks and shows what he does" (Katz, 1996, p. 90–94). As we have highlighted, it is significant that the child is present in the title of four of Ferenczi's nine most important essays published after the turning point of 1928.

Thus, among the objectives of the treatment of traumatized patients, Ferenczi advocated, inspired by Michael Balint's proposition, a "new beginning",[6] made possible by the dissolution of the crystallized

6 The expression was originally used by Balint in his presentation to the 12th International Psychoanalytic Congress in Wiesbaden, quoted by Ferenczi in the *Clinical Diary*

structure produced by traumatic progression (*cf.* Haynal, 1995). The way for working through the traumas suffered would be through regression — sustained by the transference-experience — to the magical omnipotence caused and upheld by infantile tenderness. Yet, only through the sensitive presence of the psychoanalyst would it be possible to transform the horror caused by the anguish of abandonment and defensive isolation into a true capacity to be alone and free from the lie imposed by the incorporation of persecutory objects, a condition for the creative gesture.

5.5 Thalassal regression

The matrix of the Ferenczian notion of a therapeutic function of regression is found in *Thalassa, a Theory of Genitality* (1924/1968), a Lamarckist-inspired "bioanalytical" speculation to which Ferenczi dedicated himself when he was drafted to the Hungarian army during World War I. The breadth of the issues addressed in this present work does not permit a comprehensive analysis here, for which we refer the reader to the detailed work of Luís Claudio Figueiredo (1999). Indeed, the intimate dialogue established in this period with Freud — permeated by the translation into Hungarian of the *Three Essays on the Theory of Sexuality* (Freud, 1905/1980f) and by the ideas exposed in *Overview of the Transference Neuroses* (Freud, 1915/1987) — appears to have been responsible both for the production of *Thalassa* and for the beginning of Freud's development of *Beyond the Pleasure Principle* (1920/1980j).

In the first part, dedicated to ontogeny, Ferenczi presents his thesis that coitus fulfills the fantasy of returning to the mother's womb (it is worth noting that Freud also described this fantasy, in the Wolf Man essay). The thesis would apply to all sexual beings. It reads: "I doubt not that this train of thought will find striking confirmation in the

---

(1932/1988, p. 190). In this regard, see also Gurevich (2016) and Koritar (2016).

observation of the sexual life of animals, and I regret only that I lack access to this field of knowledge" (Ferenczi, 1924/1968, p. 26). It is true that the idea that we regress daily to previously experienced modes of satisfaction was already present in the 1913 essay, dedicated to the stages of development of the sense of reality: in dreams, re-experiencing magical-hallucinatory omnipotence, in artwork, omnipotence through the help of magic gestures, and for example, in psychopathological conditions, too, regression manifests its dimension of realizing omnipotent desires. Nevertheless, it is only in the second part of *Thalassa*, dedicated to phylogenetics, that will we find the radical nature of Ferenczi's proposition regarding regressive psychical movements.

The "phylogenetic parallel" states that the stages of individual development repeat the critical moments of the adaptation of the species, going back to the great catastrophe: the drying up of the seas. Bokanowski (2000, p. 60) even points out that five years after its publication Ferenczi changed the title of the Hungarian edition to *Catastrophes in the Development of the Genital Function: A Psychoanalytic Study*. The main hypothesis presented is that sexual beings, including human beings, had to adapt to the catastrophic change from the aquatic environment to the dry environment, though a "thalassal regressive tendency" would have survived in them; or, in Ferenczi's words, "the striving towards the aquatic mode of existence abandoned in primeval times" (Ferenczi, 1924/1968, p. 52). Further, the bioanalytical conception, i.e., the one that considers the postulates of psychoanalysis for the understanding of biological processes, would dictate that all adaptive evolution not only takes place in response to the need for survival but is also the result of a *desire*. Hence Ferenczi's interest in Lamarck, in contrast to the Darwinian theory of chance in genetic mutation and evolution according to natural selection.

It is precisely this "thalassal regressive tendency" (Ferenczi, 1924/1968, p. 56) that would be at the origin of human eroticism and sexuality, since both the penetration effected by coitus and the fertilization of the egg by the sperm inside the woman's body, as well as intrauterine pregnancy, would fulfill the desire to return to the humidity that characterized primeval aquatic life.

However, it is only in the "appendix" entitled *Coitus and Sleep* that we find the most striking formulations regarding the regenerative, and even healing, role of regression. Ferenczi (1924/1968, p. 79) demonstrates a similarity between the invigorating effect of sleep and the increased capacity for achievement, which manifests itself after sexual satisfaction in coitus; both would be indebted to the plunge " into that paradisiacal life in which there is no struggle for existence but only effortless growth and increase". In morbid states, healing would also essentially take place during sleep; and, concerning falling in love, Ferenczi refers to the "miraculous healing power of love".

When reading *Thalassa*, one may recall the mythical notion of *unconditional omnipotence* lived in the intrauterine state described in "Stages in the Development of the Sense of Reality" (Ferenczi, 1913/1994d). In his bioanalytical fiction, however, Ferenczi (1924/1968) expands the ontogenetic conception of a regressive desire towards lost omnipotence by formulating a "biological unconscious" of the species that, once accessed, nourishes each individual by becoming a "source of curative and regenerative power" (Ferenczi, 1924/1968, p. 91).

As such, the experiences that perform the thalassal regression would evoke the evolutionary potential that survives in the core of each living being. Referring to healing sleep and the amorous state that leads to coitus, Ferenczi (1924/1968, p. 79) speculates that, in them, "[n]ature seems to go back to age-old generative powers and marshal these in the service of regeneration". With the hypotheses presented in *Thalassa,* the idea of a "new beginning" made possible by therapeutic regression gains supporting arguments to accompany Ferenczi's clinical postulates. The analytical setting oriented by the principle of relaxation would therefore symbolize the thalassal environment capable of promoting the recovery of the analysand's vitality.

According to Freud (1933/1964a, p. 279), by mixing "authentic discovery" and "scientific fantasy" in guessing future knowledge, *Thalassa* reveals an extraordinary intellectual "boldness". Even bolder, though, would be the derivation of an unprecedented clinical style from its hypotheses.

5.6 Epilogue: authenticity, neocatharsis, and "becoming-child"

To conclude this last chapter, I will summarize what we consider to be the crucial elements proposed to determine the goals of psychoanalytic treatment according to the theoretical-clinical contributions of Sándor Ferenczi. Since my starting point was the essay "The Problem of the Termination of the Analysis", it is worth pointing out as a last disclaimer that, if Ferenczi (1927/1994j) considers the end, and also the purpose and/or objectives, of clinical psychology to be a "problem" (*Problem*, in German), this is less due to a suggestion that analysis would actually be interminable than to the indication that reflections on the termination of analysis risk turning the entire body of psychoanalytic clinical thought upside-down, putting the psychoanalyst, not the analysand, at the pivotal center of the questions raised.

5.6.1 Authenticity

If Ferenczi believes there is no termination of analysis without overcoming the tendency to "lie" — in which lying is understood to mean the effect of identification with the aggressor that is responsible for the incorporation of the (hypocritical) disavowal coming from the sphere of the Other — one can indicate its reverse, the encounter with authenticity, as one of the primary purposes of psychoanalytic treatment. The lie corresponds, as we have seen, to the silence imposed on sensitive expression, and on the language of tenderness, that would be capable of producing meaning for the pain experienced by the traumatic intrusion. Authenticity, by contrast, entails reclaiming the joy that promotes the introjections responsible for expanding subjectivity in its movement of creating the self and the field of objects worthy of its desiring investment. This process is only possible by "the dissolution of the crystalline structure" (1927/1994j, p. 81) of character, and deconstructing the "several super-egos" (1927/1994j, p. 78) resulting from the narcissistic splitting, which impel subjectivity to a constant threat of disintegration.

As per the inspiration found in Rozenthal (2014), authenticity would effectively be the possibility of exercising, with the exuberance associated with the instinctual élan that animates the child's gesture, the child's capacity to *be* — its be-ing, in the gerund form.

5.6.2 Neocatharsis

Considering that the identification effect which takes place at the *time of disavowal* is a traumatic *progression* — through which the subject is split into a destroyed sensitive core, protected by an affectively numb facade of omniscience — the direction of the psychoanalytic treatment aims to achieve the analysand's *regression* to the earliest stages of the development of the sense of reality so that he can access his traumatized nuclei while also experiencing the magical-creative omnipotence that was damaged by the abandonment experienced at the hands of family or environment.

In "The Unwelcome Child and His Death Instinct" (1929/1994m), Ferenczi posits that the child's vital force and will to live are not very intense at the beginning of subjective experience; both depend on the quality of the encounter with adults who provide the care that ensures protection against physical and psychic violence and the consequent increase in the death instinct.

In this sense, the psychoanalyst's empathy is a condition *sine qua non* for accessing the sensitive core of the split analysand, hampered in his affective expression, and thus enabling reinstatement of the pleasure of living and the recognition of good reasons to continue existing.

5.6.3 Becoming-child

In "Confusion of Tongues between Adults and the Child" (1933/1994q), Ferenczi accurately emphasizes, through the notion of a language of tenderness, the role of the infantile way of loving (which subsists in all of us) in symbolization processes that constitute the experience of self, and in working through the affective intensities experienced in the encounter with the sexuality — the "language of passion" — of adults. His inspiration for postulating a traumatizing *confusion of tongues* was, as we have seen, the geopolitical situation of Hungary at the time, as the German language was imposed in institutions that regulated public life, relegating Magyar to designating affective and intimate experiences pertaining to family and community.

He argues that traumatized subjectivities would split and mimetically adopt the language of passion imposed by adults, at the price of losing the authenticity of their way of feeling, thinking, and acting. As a result, the clinical task would involve redeeming the evocative "word" — capacity of expression — that pertains to the language of tenderness (*cf.* Mezan, 1993); moreover, it would require the psychoanalyst's availability to share the "lesser tongue" of tenderness, capable of affecting the analysand who has been cut off from his sense of self (*cf.* Maciel, Barbosa & Carvalho, 2018). For Ferenczi, in these cases, interpretation often succeeds only in establishing a sterile dialogue with the fragment of subjectivity that is identified with the aggressor, reaching only the intelligible dimension of the subject, keeping his deadly numbness intact. More than talking *about* the child who anachronistically survives in the infantile neurosis of each analysand, it would be necessary to talk *to* the traumatized child, witnessing the unspeakable fact of his pain.

In the March 13, 1932 entry of the *Clinical Diary*, we find a development of the notion that every analysis is the analysis of a child. Ferenczi (1932/1988, p. 56) posits that at many moments, particularly when the epiphany is reached that the state of helplessness is a tragic condition of existence, the analysis is inhabited by *two children*: the patient and the psychoanalyst who, as a result of a shared fate, understand each other and establish a bond of mutual trust capable of transforming the agony caused by the threat of abandonment into a creative impulse.

Thus, as we predictably circle back to the introductory lines of this chapter, it can be understood without much difficulty that among the main obstacles to a psychoanalytic treatment reaching its goals is the psychoanalyst's resistance *to his own capacity for becoming-child.* Ferenczi (1932/1988) is even more precise in naming it: the greatest resistance to analysis is the psychoanalyst's fear of madness that arises in coming into contact with childhood trauma.

Consequently, if psychoanalysis imposes a single fundamental rule on those who resort to it, namely free association (which forces them to face the strangeness of being in contact with the repressed unconscious and the agony of regressing to their split traumatic nuclei), the counterpart required of the analyst is that he must carry his own analysis as far as possible — far enough to have the necessary sensitivity to uphold the principles of the ethics of care that legitimize the psychoanalytic experience.

6. Conclusion

Among Chuang-Tzu's many skills, he was an expert draftsman. The king asked him to draw a crab. Chuang-Tzu replied that he needed five years, a country house, and twelve servants. Five years later the drawing was still not begun. "I need another five years", said Chuang-Tzu. The king granted them. At the end of these ten years, Chuang-Tzu took up his brush and, in an instant, with a single stroke, he drew a crab, the most perfect crab ever seen.

(Italo Calvino, 1988, p. 54)

The analogy between the work of the psychoanalyst and the art of the sculptor has been in the minds of psychoanalysts for over a century. In "On Psychotherapy", Freud (1905[1904]/2017a) uses the formulas employed by Leonardo da Vinci to differentiate painting from sculpture to define a similarly radical distinction between the psychoanalytic method and the technique of suggestion. In this construction, he proposes that suggestion operates *per via di porre* ("by way of adding"): that is to say, in the same way that the painter adds patches of paint to the empty canvas, by using the technique of suggestion the therapist imposes prohibitions or injunctions on the patient in an attempt to combat his pathological ideation and symptoms. The psychoanalyst, by contrast, acts *per via di levare* ("by way of removing"): instead of adding things, he seeks to elucidate, through interpretation, the components that constitute the neurosis, eliminating them in the same way that the sculptor removes fragments of rough stone to give his work its final shape.

Although inspiring, the similarity with sculpture is evidently insufficient to express the complexity of the exercise of psychoanalysis. At least, that is what I have tried to demonstrate throughout the chapters that make up this volume. However, much of the psychoanalytic community still takes the reference to sculpture at face value. Simply to state that psychoanalysis operates *per via di levare* would be to ignore the entire journey undertaken first by Freud, then by Ferenczi, with the active technique. Furthermore, it would be to ignore all the efforts made by Ferenczi in treating "difficult patients", who bear the consequences of traumatic disavowal in their psyche. His empathic clinical style teaches us that you don't just analyze with the hammer; as proposed elsewhere (Kupermann, 2017), one must also have regard for the delicacy of the chisel.

In this sense, to insist more than a century later on the opposition between *via di porre* and *via di levare* in psychoanalysis is to cling to the idea that the true struggle still lies outside its heuristic field; it is to continue to believe that the threats to the development of psychoanalysis stem only from the resistance raised by the culture. The twist operated by Ferenczi since the 1920s, on the other hand, points to another, much less paranoiac perspective: the greatest resistances to the development of psychoanalysis have been in the ways in which psychoanalysts defend themselves from the impact of the clinical encounter on their own subjectivities.

Indeed, the path described in "The Further Development of an Active Therapy in Psycho-Analysis" (Ferenczi, 1920/1994f) demonstrates that what the excessive attachment of analysts to the technique governed by the principles of neutrality and abstinence revealed was less a desirable ethical-methodological rigor than a shield against the horror witnessed by their analysands. This in practice would lead to reproduction, in the transference, of the *disavowal,* thus making the analytic situation a cause of re-traumatization. In this context, the *via di levare* was mistaken for the hypocrisy denounced by Ferenczi in his *Clinical Diary*. If the "Teflon psychoanalyst" does not add any affective element to the setting, it is because nothing adheres to him: he is immune to the analysand's affects, ultimately becoming truly insensitive. This, according to Ferenczi, is the source of the most damaging resistances to psychoanalysis.

Throughout the itinerary of this investigation, I have sought to demonstrate that the formulation of neocatharsis reveals that the psychoanalyst's work necessarily evolves by way of the *sensitive path of working-through*. However, it should be clarified that I do not intend to come up with a "third way" as a compromise solution for the conflicts between the different conceptions of psychoanalysis that currently permeate the psychoanalytic field. Inspired by the Utraquist[1] method proposed by Ferenczi in *Thalassa*, which combines seemingly heterogeneous elements, escaping the ubiquitous binary logic of scientific rationality, I demonstrate that psychoanalysis operates *per via di levare* and, also, *per via di porre*, according to the direction presented by the analytical encounter. Both alternatives are nevertheless guided by the sensitive way of working-through, which plays the pivotal role that sustains the clinical exercise.

As formulated by Luís Claudio Figueiredo (2000), who was inspired by the "Aunt Sally" figure evoked by Ferenczi — the doll that recovers from successive blows — the psychoanalyst sways back and forth between instigation and reserve, two stances that guide his indispensably sensitive presence, always nuanced according to

---

1 The Latin word *utraque* means "one and the other".

the inclination of the "here and now" of transference. Insisting on a paradoxical logic, more akin to Ferenczi's thinking, we could say that analysts, in their practice, also sway back and forth between activity and passivity, love and hate, agony and serenity, elasticity and limit, whereas the thermometer capable of measuring the temperature of the analytical setting can only be guided by the metric of empathy.

If Ferenczi was called the *enfant terrible* of psychoanalysis, it is because reading his texts caused a discomfort similar to that caused by the naughty child who does not hesitate to reveal when the king is naked. His work effectively shook the three supporting pillars of psychoanalytic thinking: metapsychology/psychopathology, clinical theory, and psychoanalytic ethics.

Shortly after his first meeting with Freud, Ferenczi published "Introjection and Transference", in which he presented to the psychoanalytic community the key notion of his theory of the subjective constitution. The emphasis placed by Ferenczi on the period of indiscrimination between the child's self — always corporeal — and the objects of the world allowed him to express the mimetic-sensitive dimension through which the subject enunciates the language of tenderness, creating the meanings that guide his libidinal investments. Formalized in the famous "Confusion of Tongues between Adults and the Child", the language of tenderness is, therefore, the chosen means of expression of a child's omnipotence, the driving force of the expansive movement of subjectivity and the constitution of his symbolic relations.

However, the condition for the introjective movement to be possible is the experience of *passive object-love* provided by environmental adaptation. In this sense, the "unwelcome" child is abandoned in the face of the destructive potential of Thanatos. His authentic gesture having been damaged, he resorts to identification with the aggressor, adopting a narcissistic split between an intelligible part, representing the incorporated object, and his devastated sensitive core. According to what Ferenczi found in his clinical practice, the "difficult" patient then chooses the pathway of masochistic submission, to avoid an even more unbearable displeasure, the agony caused by traumatic abandonment (*cf.* Ferenczi, 1926/1993b).

The main clinical consequence of Ferenczi's formulations on traumatogenesis was the understanding that it is the psychoanalytic method, and each psychoanalyst in particular, that should adapt to the time, rhythm, and uniqueness of each analysand's suffering, not the other way around. Listening to patients who were considered unanalyzable demonstrated the "flipside" of clinical practice: the limits of the standard technique, governed by the three-factor structure of free association, the principle of abstinence in transference, and the psychoanalyst's interpretation, a discovery that gave these patients a new status as subjects traumatized by disavowal and breach of trust. Treating them required creating an *empathic style,* attuned to the aesthetic nuances of the clinical encounter, making the analytic setting more elastic, as inspired by clinical psychology with children, which at the time was engaging the attention of psychoanalysts.

The trilogy that caused what I have called the *turning point of 1928* definitively sealed the link between psychoanalysis and an *ethics of care,* governed by the principles of hospitality towards the *infans* (who does not speak the adults' language of passion), empathy, and the analyst's health. The principle of relaxation, proposed by Ferenczi shortly afterward, made it possible for the analysand to achieve the thalassal regression and the expression of his *capacity for becoming-child,* favoring the practice of sharing of "play" with the analyst. As a result, it was possible for the analysand to evoke his earliest traumatic experiences, and to achieve, often for the first time in his life, the liberty ("irresponsibility of childhood") required for the manifestation of his creativity. The elements accessed through analysis informed the psychoanalyst's constructions, providing the analysand with the conviction of the authenticity of his testimony, indispensable for working through his traumatic nuclei and, finally, for producing a singular meaning for his suffering.

Ferenczi, however, quickly realized that the condition for the *time of testimony* to return, in the analytic setting, was the psychoanalyst's sensitive availability, often shaken by the intensity of the affects that permeate the analytic encounter, with the risk that they may lead the analyst to *deauthorize* the countertransference, adopting a hypocritical stance in relation to the analysand. Thus, the *second fundamental rule* of psychoanalysis formulated by Ferenczi was that the psychoanalyst should have completed his own analysis or taken it as far as possible — faithful to the Freudian principle that an analysis only goes as far as the psychoanalyst's own analysis.

Accused of letting his *furor sanandi* compromise his technical rigor, Ferenczi's true obsession seems to have been the encounter with the end of analysis; his own, above all. Having complained that Freud had not let his analysis go forward, since he did not recognize his negative transference, Ferenczi experimented in the last years of his life with the "mutual analysis" described in his *Clinical Diary*, especially with his patient Elisabeth Severn, also a therapist (*cf.* Rudnytsky, 2015). The mutuality practiced (in very rare cases) by Ferenczi did not mean an arbitrary practice of self-disclosure on the part of the psychoanalyst; it was, above all, a question of *sincerity,* as opposed to the hypocrisy adopted by many of his colleagues when they appeared to show a friendly benevolence toward their analysands, in situations where in fact they ought to be expressing their own hostility. As a result, in one of the episodes reported in the *Clinical Diary*, after a few comments from his analysand, Ferenczi recognized his own misogyny which, once analyzed, allowed for Severn's treatment to continue.

A panoramic analysis of the clinical journey undertaken by Ferenczi will show that, in his understanding, the primary objective of the analysis is to help the analysand get rid of the incorporated object that is acting as a tyrannical superego, thus enabling the encounter with his authenticity. But achieving this end required providing the analysand with the opportunity to exercise, often for the first time, the ambivalence expressed by the negative transference, actively supporting his discomfort, through resistance *within* the clinical encounter. This results in neocatharsis, which is capable of awakening affects of vitality in the analysand, constrained as he was by the action of his death instinct.

It was precisely the definition of a psychoanalytic practice unequivocally linked to an ethics of care that made Ferenczi the precursor of generations of psychoanalysts attentive to the quality of the intersubjective encounter for the success of the clinical endeavor, among which we can list Melanie Klein, Michael Balint, and Donald Woods Winnicott, as indicated by Luiz Eduardo Prado de Oliveira (2011). Jacques Lacan was also strongly influenced by Ferenczi with regard to questioning (i) the limits of the analytical setting and of the work of the analyst — including breaking the rigidity of the chronological time of the sessions; (ii) the active technique and, above all, (iii) "The Problem of the Termination of the Analysis".

But it was certainly Winnicott who revealed the greatest resonances with Ferenczian thought. His environmentalist perspective, anchored in the figure of the *good enough mother*, is the amplified version of the concept of the family's adaptation to the child, which inaugurated the turning point of 1928 and reaffirms the affiliation of psychoanalysis to the field of the ethics of care. Further, recognition of two principles, (i) the progress of trauma and (ii) the basic split of the personality between a true and a false self, impelled Winnicott to admit two components — regression to dependence, and playing — as guiding factors of his own clinical style. Let it be said, though, that research on Ferenczi's influence on Lacan and Winnicott would certainly require independent efforts, other than those on which this present investigation has centered.

As we approach the conclusion of this work, I acknowledge that I continue to owe the reader an incursion into the extensive and fruitful universe of the correspondence established between Freud and Ferenczi over twenty-five years of relationship, organized by Falzeder, Brabant, and Giampieri (1994; 1995). I also believe that the *Clinical Diary* deserves a full independent analysis; I have used it only incidentally, to highlight some of the ideas that supported our argument. In this regard, I can only say that I hope that academic life and clinical practice will enable us to have the health and time for new endeavors, with the intention of repairing the gaps left by this work.

In a letter addressed to humorist Fréderic Karinthy, who had published an article criticizing psychoanalysis, Ferenczi (1924/1993a) reminds him that years before, Karinthy himself, enthusiastic about Freud's innovation, had pointed out the difference between a science that "awakens humanity", by seeking the truth, from another that "puts it to sleep", avoiding "disturbing the quietude of the drowsy world".

On this basis, we would have two kinds of scientists: those who disturb by awakening, and those who watch over humanity's sleep. Ferenczi concludes by provoking the recipient of his letter: "I am now the one who has not abandoned the ranks of those who awaken" (Ferenczi, 1924/1993a).

I believe that at the end of this journey, the reader will have gathered sufficient evidence that Ferenczi thought and practiced, as much as possible, a psychoanalysis that carries the gift of awakening and rebirth.

References[1]

Agamben, G. (2002). *Homo sacer: o poder soberano e a vida nua.* Editora UFMG.

Agamben, G. (2008). *O que resta de Auschwitz: o arquivo e o testemunho (Homo Sacer III).* Boitempo.

Andersen, H. C. (1837). *The Emperor's New Clothes.* Retrieved 22 Feb 2024, from https://andersen.sdu.dk/vaerk/hersholt/TheEmperors-NewClothes_e.html

Aron, L., & Harris, A. (Eds.). (1993). *The legacy of Sándor Ferenczi.* The Analytic Press.

Avello, J. J. (2013). *L'ile des reves de Sándor Ferenczi: rien que la pulsion de vie.* CapagnePremiere.

1 For an extensive list of books and papers inspired by the work of Sándor Ferenczi, I refer the reader to the website of the ISFN (*International Sándor Ferenczi Network*), https://www.sandorferenczi.org/publications/books-and-articles-inspired-by-ferenczi/. The list of Brazilian authors was initially created by Eugênio Canesin Dal Molin and Haydée Christinne Kahtuni for the *Ferenczi Renaissance Archives* and updated for the ISFN by Eugênio Canesin Dal Molin.

Bakhtin, M. (1996). *A cultura popular na Idade Média e no Renascimento: o contexto de Francois Rabelais*. Edunb-Hucitec.

Balint, M. (1948). On the psycho-analytic training system. *International Journal of Psychoanalysis*, *29*(3), 163–173.

Balint, M. (1954). Analytic training and training analysis. *International Journal of Psychoanalysis*, *35*(2), 157–162.

Balint, M. (1969). Trauma and object relationship. *International Journal of Psycho-analysis*, *50*(4), 429–435.

Balint, M. (1994). Character analysis and new beginning. In: M. Balint, *Primary love and psycho-analytic technique*. Karnac Books. (Original work published 1932)

Balint, M. (2014). *A falha básica: aspectos terapêuticos da regressão*. Zagodoni.

Barbosa, M. N. P., & Kupermann, D. (2016). Quem testemunha pelas testemunhas? Traumatismo e sublimação em Primo Levi. *Psicologia USP*, *27*(1), 31–40. https://dx.doi.org/10.1590/0103-6564D20150013

Bastos, J. G. S. (2018). *A estética do traumático: atenção a sujeitos em situação de violência e reações profissionais* (Doctoral dissertation, Pontifícia Universidade Católica de São Paulo).

Benigni, R. (Diretor). (1997). *La vita è bella* [DVD]. Miramax; Melampo Cinematografica; Caravan Pictures; Cecchi Gori Group; Cecchi Gori Pictures.

Benjamin, J. (1988). *Bonds of love: psychoanalysis, feminism, and the problem of domination*. (Verso, p. 12). Pantheon.

Benjamin, W. (1986). O narrador. In *Magia e técnica, arte e política: ensaios sobre literatura e história da cultura* (2a ed., S. P. Rouanet, trad., Obras Escolhidas, v. 1). Brasiliense.

Benjamin, W. (2002). Experiência. In *Reflexões sobre a criança, o brinquedo e a educação*. Editora 34. (Original work published 1913)

Berman, E. (1996). Review essay: the Ferenczi renaissance. *Psychoanalytic Dialogues, 6*(3), 391–411.

Bernardes, A. C. (2002). A segunda regra fundamental: um comentário sobre o Ferenczi de Lacan. *Agora: Estudos em Teoria Psicanalitica, 5*(2), 311–316. https://dx.doi.org/10.1590/S1516-14982002000200007.

Bertolucci, B. (1993). *Little Buddha* [DVD]. Miramax; Recorded Picture Company; Ciby 2000.

Birman, J. (2014a). Continuidades, descontinuidades, esgarçamentos. In *Arquivo e memória da experiência psicanalítica: Ferenczi antes de Freud, depois de Lacan*. Contra Capa.

Birman, J. (2014b). Desatar com atos. In *Arquivo e memória da experiência psicanalítica: Ferenczi antes de Freud, depois de Lacan*. Contra Capa.

Bokanowski, T. (2000). *Sándor Ferenczi*. Via Lettera.

Bonomi, C. (1998). Ferenczi and contemporary psychoanalysis [Editorial]. *International Forum Psychoanalysis, 7*(4), 181–185.

Borgogno, F. (2015). Ferenczi, the "introjective analyst". In A. Harris & S. Kuchuck (Eds.), *The legacy of Sándor Ferenczi: from ghost to ancestor*. Routledge.

Botella, C., & Botella, S. (2002). *Irrepresentável, mais além da representacao*. Editora Criação Humana.

Breuer, J., & Freud, S. (1955). Studies on hysteria. In *The standard edition of the complete psychological works of Sigmund Freud* (J. Strachey, trad., Vol. II). London: The Hogarth Press. (Original work published 1893–1895)

Brunswick, R. M. (1981). Supplement a "l'extrait de l'histoire d'une nevrose infantile" de Freud. In M. Gardiner (Org.), *L'Homme aux loups par ses psychanalystes et par lui-meme* (M. Bonaparte, trad., p. 268–316). Gallimard. (Original work published 1928)

Buber, M. (1995). *Histórias do rabi*. Perspectiva.

Cabré, L. M. (2017). Introducción. In L. C. Cabre (Coord.), *Autenticidad y reciprocidad: un diálogo com Ferenczi*. Biebel.

Calvino, I. (1988). *Six memos for the next millennium*. Harvard University Press.

Centre Georges Pompidou. *Maryan S. Maryan's Notebooks*. Retrieved 22 Feb 2024, from https://www.centrepompidou.fr/fr/recherche/oeuvres?terms=maryan%20carnet

Chaui, M. (1987). Amizade, recusa do servir. In E. La Boetie, *Discurso da servidão voluntária*. Brasiliense.

Chaves, E. (2001). A paciência no trabalho analítico. *Pulsional: Revista de Psicanálise*, *14*(147), 5–11.

Cintra, E. M. U., Tamburrino, G., & Ribeiro, M. F. R. (Orgs.). (2017). *Para além da contratransferência: o analista implicado*. Zagodoni.

Costa, J. F. (2000). O mito psicanalítico do desamparo. *Agora: Estudos em Teoria Psicanalítica*, *3*(1), 25–46.

Dal Molin, E. C. (2016). *O terceiro tempo do trauma*. Perspectiva/Fapesp.

Dallazen, L. (2017). *A perlaboração da contratransferência e o processo de alucinação do psicanalista como recursos das construções em análise* (Doctoral dissertation, Instituto de Psicologia da Universidade de São Paulo). doi:10.11606/T.47.2018.tde-19042018-145618

Dean-Gomes, G. (2019). *Budapeste, Viena e Wiesbaden: o percurso do pensamento clínico-teórico de Sándor*. Blucher.

Derrida, J. (2000). Foreigner question. In J. Derrida & A. Dufourmantelle, *Anne Dufourmantelle invites Jacques Derrida to respond of hospitality*. Stanford University Press.

Falzeder, E., Brabant, E., & Giampieri, P. (Eds.). (1994). *Sigmund Freud & Sándor Ferenczi: correspondência* (Vol. 1, Tomo 1 (1908–1911). Imago.

Falzeder, E., Brabant, E., & Giampieri, P. (Eds.). (1995). *Sigmund Freud & Sándor Ferenczi: correspondência* (Vol. 1, Tomo 2 (1912–1914). Imago.

Ferenczi, S. (1931). Kinderanalysen mit Erwachsenen. *Internationale Zeitschrift fur Psychoanalyse, 17*(2), 161–175.

Ferenczi, S. (1933). Sprachverwirrung zwischen den Erwachsenen und dem Kind: (Die Sprache der Zartlichkeit und der Leidenschaft). *Internationale Zeitschrift fur Psychoanalyse, 19*(1–2), 5–15.

Ferenczi, S. (1939). Die Elastizitat der psychoanalytischen Technik (1927–28). In *Bausteine zur Psychoananalyse. III. Arbeiten aus den Jahren 1908–1933* (p. 383). Hans Huber. (Original work published 1928)

Ferenczi, S. (1968). Coitus and sleep. In *Thalassa: a theory of genitality*. The Norton Library. (Original work published 1924)

Ferenczi, S. (1982). Elasticite de la technique psychanalytique. In *Psychanalyse IV: Ouevres completes 1927–1933*. Payot. (Original work published 1928)

Ferenczi, S. (1988). *The clinical diary of Sándor Ferenczi*. Harvard University Press. (Original work published 1932)

Ferenczi, S. (1991a). Do alcance da ejaculação precoce. In *Psicanálise I* (Obras completas, 1). Martins Fontes. (Original work published 1908)

Ferenczi, S. (1991b). Sobre a história do movimento psicanalítico. In *Psicanálise I* (Obras completas, 1). Martins Fontes. (Original work published 1911)

Ferenczi, S. (1991c). O conceito de introjeção. In *Psicanálise I* (Obras completas, 1). Martins Fontes. (Original work published 1912)

Ferenczi, S. (1992a). Ontogênese dos símbolos. In *Psicanálise II* (Obras completas de Sándor Ferenczi, 2). Martins Fontes. (Original work published 1913)

Ferenczi, S. (1992b). Dois tipos de neurose de guerra. In *Psicanálise II* (Obras completas de Sándor Ferenczi, 2). Martins Fontes. (Original work published 1916)

Ferenczi, S. (1992c). As patoneuroses. In *Psicanálise II* (Obras completas de Sándor Ferenczi, 2). Martins Fontes. (Original work published 1917)

Ferenczi, S. (1993a). Ciência que adormece, ciência que desperta (carta a Frederic Karinthy). In *Psicanálise III* (Obras completas de Sándor Ferenczi, 3). Martins Fontes. (Original work published 1924)

Ferenczi, S. (1993b). O problema da afirmação do desprazer (progressos no conhecimento do sentido de realidade). In *Psicanálise III* (Obras completas de Sándor Ferenczi, 3). Martins Fontes. (Original work published 1926)

Ferenczi, S. (1993c). *Psicanálise III*. Martins Fontes.

Ferenczi, S. (1994a). Introjection and transference. In *First contributions to psycho-analysis* (Vol. 1). Karnac Classics. (Original work published 1909)

Ferenczi, S. (1994b). On obscene words. In *First contributions to psycho-analysis* (Vol. 1). Karnac Classics. (Original work published 1911)

Ferenczi, S. (1994c). On eye symbolism. In *First contributions to psycho-analysis* (Vol. 1). Karnac Classics. (Original work published 1913)

Ferenczi, S. (1994d). Stages in the development of the sense of reality. In *First contributions to psycho-analysis* (Vol. 1). Karnac Classics. (Original work published 1913)

Ferenczi, S. (1994e). Technical difficulties in the analysis of a case of hysteria. In *Further contributions to the theory and technique of psycho-analysis* (Vol. 2). Karnac Classics. (Original work published 1919)

Ferenczi, S. (1994f). The further development of an active therapy in psychoanalysis. In *Further contributions to the theory and technique of psycho-analysis* (Vol. 2). Karnac Classics. (Original work published 1920)

Ferenczi, S. (1994g). The dream of the 'clever baby'. In *Further contributions to the theory and technique of psycho-analysis* (Vol. 2). Karnac Classics. (Original work published 1923)

Ferenczi, S. (1994h). On forced phantasies. In *Further contributions to the theory and technique of psycho-analysis* (Vol. 2). Karnac Classics. (Original work published 1924)

Ferenczi, S. (1994i). Contra-indications to the 'active' psycho-analytical technique. In *Further contributions to the theory and technique of psycho-analysis* (Vol. 2). Karnac Classics. (Original work published 1925)

Ferenczi, S. (1994j). The problem of the termination of the analysis. In *Final contributions to the problem and methods of psychoanalysis* (Vol. 3). Karnac Classics. (Original work published 1927)

Ferenczi, S. (1994k). The adaptation of the family to the child. In *Final contributions to the problem and methods of psycho-analysis* (Vol. 3). Karnac Classics. (Original work published 1928)

Ferenczi, S. (1994l). The elasticity of psycho-analytic technique. In *Final contributions to the problem and methods of psychoanalysis* (Vol. 3). Karnac Classics. (Original work published 1928)

Ferenczi, S. (1994m). The unwelcome child and his death instinct. In *Final contributions to the problem and methods of psychoanalysis* (Vol. 3). Karnac Classics. (Original work published 1929)

Ferenczi, S. (1994n). The principle of relaxation and neocatharsis. In *Final contributions to the problem and methods of psychoanalysis* (Vol. 3). Karnac Classics. (Original work published 1930)

Ferenczi, S. (1994o). Child-analysis in the analysis of adults. In *Final contributions to the problem and methods of psycho-analysis* (Vol. 3). Karnac Classics. (Original work published 1931)

Ferenczi, S. (1994p). On Shock. In Final contributions to the problem and methods of psycho-analysis (Vol. 3). Karnac Classics. (Original work published 1932)

Ferenczi, S. (1994q). Confusion of tongues between adults and the child. In *Final contributions to the problem and methods of psychoanalysis* (Vol. 3). Karnac Classics. (Original work published 1933)

Figueiredo, L. C. (1999). *Palavras cruzadas entre Freud e Ferenczi.* Escuta.

Figueiredo, L. C. (2000). Presença, implicação e reserva. In L. C. Figueiredo & N. E. Coelho Jr. *Ética e técnica em psicanálise.* Escuta.

Figueiredo, L. C. (2008). *Verleugnung:* a desautorização do processo perceptivo. In *Psicanálise: elementos para a clínica contemporânea.* Escuta.

Figueiredo, L. C. (2009). *As diversas faces do cuidar: novos ensaios de psicanálise contemporânea.* Escuta.

Figueiredo, L. C. (2014). *Cuidado, saúde e cultura: trabalhos psíquicos e criatividade na situação analisante.* Escuta.

Floresta de Miranda, H. (2012). Confusão das línguas: eficiência e deficiências da tradução. In J. Verztman, R. Herzog, T. Pinheiro & F. Pacheco-Ferreira (Orgs.), *Sofrimentos narcísicos.* Cia de Freud.

Foucault, M. (2000). *O que é um autor?* Veja. (Original work published 1969)

Franco, W. A. C. (2018). *Os lugares da psicanálise: a inscrição clínica e cultural do pensamento psicanalítico* (Doctoral dissertation, Instituto de Psicologia da Universidade de São Paulo). http://www.teses.usp.br/teses/disponiveis/47/47133/tde-19122018-095103/

Frankel, J. (2017). Ferenczi's evolving conception of narcissistic pathology and its basis in trauma. *American Journal of Psychoanalysis, 77*(3), 213–222.

Freud, S. (1955a). Psychotherapy of hysteria. In J. Breuer & S. Freud, *Studies on hysteria (1893–1895)*. (J. Strachey, trad., The standard edition of the complete psychological works of Sigmund Freud, Vol. II). The Hogarth Press. (Original work published 1893–1895)

Freud, S. (1955b). From the history of an infantile neurosis. In *The standard edition of the complete psychological works of Sigmund Freud* (J. Strachey, trad., Vol. XVII). The Hogarth Press. (Original work published 1918[1914])

Freud, S. (1955c). Turnings in the ways of psycho-analytic therapy. In *From the history of an infantile neurosis*. (J. Strachey, trad., The standard edition of the complete psychological works of Sigmund Freud, Vol. XVII). The Hogarth Press. (Original work published 1919[1918])

Freud, S. (1957a). 'Wild' psycho-analysis. In S. Freud, *Leonardo da Vinci and a Memory of his childhood* (J. Strachey, trad., The standard edition of the complete psychological works of Sigmund Freud, Vol. XI). The Hogarth Press. (Original work published 1910)

Freud, S. (1957b). Instincts and their vicissitudes. In S. Freud, *Papers on metapsychology* (J. Strachey, trad., The standard edition of the complete psychological works of Sigmund Freud, Vol. XIV). The Hogarth Press. (Original work published 1915)

Freud, S. (1958a). Recommendations to physicians practicing psychoanalysis. In *Papers on technique* (J. Strachey, trad., The standard edition of the complete psychological works of Sigmund Freud, Vol. XII). The Hogarth Press. (Original work published 1912)

Freud, S. (1958b). The dynamics of transference. In *Papers on technique* (J. Strachey, trad., The standard edition of the complete psychological works of Sigmund Freud, Vol. XII). The Hogarth Press. (Original work published 1912)

Freud, S. (1958c). Further recommendations on the technique of psychoanalysis II: remembering, repeating, and working-through. In *Papers on technique* (J. Strachey, trad., The standard edition of the complete psychological works of Sigmund Freud, Vol. XII). The Hogarth Press. (Original work published 1914)

Freud, S. (1961). Dr. Sándor Ferenczi (on his 50th birthday). In *The ego and the id.* (J. Strachey, trad., The standard edition of the complete psychological works of Sigmund Freud, Vol. XIX). The Hogarth Press. (Original work published 1923)

Freud, S. (1964a). Sándor Ferenczi. In *New introductory lectures on psycho-analysis (1933[1932])* (J. Strachey, trad., The standard edition of the complete psychological works of Sigmund Freud, Vol. XXII). The Hogarth Press. (Original work published 1933)

Freud, S. (1964b). Analysis terminable and interminable. In *Moses and Monotheism: three essays.* (J. Strachey, trad., The standard edition of the complete psychological works of Sigmund Freud, Vol. XXIII). The Hogarth Press. (Original work published 1937)

Freud, S. (1964c). Constructions in analysis. In *An outline of psycho-analysis.* (J. Strachey, trad., The standard edition of the complete psychological works of Sigmund Freud, Vol. XXIII). The Hogarth Press. (Original work published 1937)

Freud, S. (1966a). Extracts from the Fliess papers – letter 69. In *Pre-psycho-analytic publications and unpublished drafts (1886–1889).* (J. Strachey, trad., The standard edition of the complete psychological works of Sigmund Freud, Vol. I). The Hogarth Press. (Original work published 1897)

Freud, S. (1966b). Project for a scientific psychology. In *Pre-psycho-analytic publications and unpublished drafts.* (J. Strachey, trad., The standard edition of the complete psychological works of Sigmund Freud, Vol. I). The Hogarth Press. (Original work published 1950[1895])

Freud, S. (1980a). As neuropsicoses de defesa. Primeiras publicações psicanalíticas. In *Edição standard brasileira das obras psicológicas completas de Sigmund Freud* (Vol. 3). Imago. (Original work published 1894)

Freud, S. (1980b). Novos comentários sobre as neuropsicoses de defesa. Primeiras publicações psicanalíticas In *Edição standard brasileira das obras psicológicas completas de Sigmund Freud* (Vol. 3). Imago. (Original work published 1896)

Freud, S. (1980c). Lembranças encobridoras. Primeiras publicações psicanalíticas. In *Edição standard brasileira das obras psicológicas completas de Sigmund Freud* (Vol. 3). Imago. (Original work published 1899)

Freud, S. (1980d). A interpretação de sonhos (1) (1900). In *Edição standard brasileira das obras psicológicas completas de Sigmund Freud* (Vol. 4). Imago. (Original work published 1900)

Freud, S. (1980e). A interpretação de sonhos (2) (1900–1901). In *Edição standard brasileira das obras psicológicas completas de Sigmund Freud* (Vol. 5). Imago. (Original work published 1900)

Freud, S. (1980f). Um caso de histeria, três ensaios sobre sexualidade e outros trabalhos (1901–1905). In *Edição standard brasileira das obras psicológicas completas de Sigmund Freud* (Vol. 7). Imago. (Original work published 1905)

Freud, S. (1980g). Os chistes e sua relação com o inconsciente. In *Edição standard brasileira das obras psicológicas completas de Sigmund Freud* (Vol. 8). Imago. (Original work published 1905)

Freud, S. (1980h). Formulações sobre os dois princípios do funcionamento mental. In *Edição standard brasileira das obras psicológicas completas de Sigmund Freud* (Vol. 12). Imago. (Original work published 1911)

Freud, S. (1980i). Introdução a psicanálise e as neuroses de guerra. História de uma neurose infantil e outros trabalhos (1917–1918).

In *Edição standard brasileira das obras psicológicas completas de Sigmund Freud* (Vol. 17). Imago. (Original work published 1919)

Freud, S. (1980j). Além do princípio de prazer, psicologia de grupo e outros trabalhos (1920–1922). In *Edição standard brasileira das obras psicológicas completas de Sigmund Freud* (Vol. 18). Imago. (Original work published 1920)

Freud, S. (1980k). Sonhos e telepatia In *Edição standard brasileira das obras psicológicas completas de Sigmund Freud* (Vol. 18). Imago, 1980. (Original work published 1922)

Freud, S. (1980l). O problema econômico do masoquismo. O ego e o Id e outros trabalhos (1923–1925). In *Edição standard brasileira das obras psicológicas completas de Sigmund Freud* (Vol. 19). Imago. (Original work published 1924)

Freud, S. (1980m). Um estudo autobiográfico, Inibições, sintomas e ansiedade: a questão da análise leiga e outros trabalhos. In *Edição standard brasileira das obras psicológicas completas de Sigmund Freud* (Vol. 20). Imago. (Original work published 1926)

Freud, S. (1980n). Fetichismo. O futuro de uma ilusão, o mal-estar na civilização e outros trabalhos (1927–1931). *Edição standard brasileira das obras psicológicas completas de Sigmund Freud* (Vol. 21). Imago. (Original work published 1927)

Freud, S. (1980o). Dostoievski e o parricídio. O futuro de uma ilusão, o mal-estar na civilização e outros trabalhos (1927–1931) In *Edição standard brasileira das obras psicológicas completas de Sigmund Freud* (Vol. 21). Imago. (Original work published 1928[1927])

Freud, S. (1980p). O mal-estar na civilização. O futuro de uma ilusão, o mal-estar na civilização e outros trabalhos (1927–1931). In *Edição standard brasileira das obras psicológicas completas de Sigmund Freud* (Vol. 21). Imago. (Original work published 1930[1929])

Freud, S. (1980q). Psicanálise e telepatia. In *Edição standard brasileira das obras psicológicas completas de Sigmund Freud* (Vol. 18). Imago. (Original work published 1941[1921])

Freud, S. (1987). *Neuroses de transferência: uma síntese*. Imago. (Original work published 1915)

Freud, S. (2017a). Sobre a psicoterapia. In *Fundamentos da clínica psicanalítica* (C. Dornbusch, trad., Obras incompletas de Sigmund Freud, Vol. 6). Autêntica, 2017. (Original work published 1905[1904])

Freud, S. (2017b). Observações sobre o amor transferencial. In S. Freud, *Fundamentos da clínica psicanalítica* (C. Dornbusch, trad., Obras incompletas de Sigmund Freud, Vol. 6). Autêntica. (Original work published 1915[1914])

Freymann, J-R. (2009). Lacan utilisait-il la technique active de Ferenczi? In L. Joseph. (Ed.). *Ferenczi apres Lacan*. Hermann Editeurs.

Galdi, G. (1996). *"Terrorism of suffering" type of transference and countertransference: an analytic perspective inspired by Ferenczi's Clinical diary.* Work presented at the American Institute for Psychoanalysis in New York, unpublished paper.

Gardiner, M. (Org.). (1981). *L'Homme aux Loups par ses psychanalystes et par lui-meme*. Gallimard.

Gay, P. (1989). *Uma vida para o nosso tempo*. Companhia das Letras.

Glicenstein, M. (1992). Ferenczi et le savoir des enfants. *Le Coq-Heron*, (125), 49–52.

Goldfajn, D. S., Martins, K. P. H., & Kupermann, D. (2018). As contribuições teórico-clínicas de Sándor Ferenczi. In A. E. A. Antúnez & G. Safra (Orgs.). *Psicologia clínica: da graduação à pós-graduação*. Atheneu.

Gondar, J. (2012). Ferenczi como pensador político. *Cadernos de Psicanálise*, 34(27), 193–210.

Gondar, J. (2017). As coisas nas palavras: Ferenczi e a linguagem. In E. S. Reis & J. Gondar, *Com Ferenczi: clínica, subjetivação, política*. 7 Letras.

Gondar, J., & Antonello, D. F. (2016). O analista como testemunha. *Psicologia USP*, *27*(1), 16–23. https://dx.doi.org/10.1590/0103-6564D20150010

Green, A. (2005). *Key ideas for a contemporary psychoanalysis. Misrecognition and recognition of the unconscious*. Routledge.

Grosskurth, P. (1991). *The secret ring: Freud's inner circle and the politics of psychoanalysis*. Addison-Wesley/Addison Wesley Longman.

Gurevich, H. (2016). Orpha, Orphic functions, and the Orphic analyst: Winnicott's "Regression to Dependence" in the language of Ferenczi. *American Journal of Psychoanalysis*, *76*, 322–340.

Gurfinkel, D. (2017). *Relações de objeto*. Blucher.

Halasz, A. (1992). La conception psychanalytique de l'enfant et l'analyse d'enfant em Hongrie avant la Seconde Guerre Mondiale. *Le Coq-Heron*, (125), 40–44.

Hanns, L. A. (1996). *Dicionário comentado do alemão de Freud*. Imago.

Haynal, A. (1995). *A técnica em questão: controvérsias em psicanálise: de Freud e Ferenczi a Michel Balint*. Casa do Psicologo/Clínica Roberto Azevedo.

Honneth, A. (2009). *Luta por reconhecimento: a gramática moral dos conflitos sociais*. Editora 34.

Izcovitch, L. (2009). La psychanalyse didactique: Lacan lecteur de Ferenczi. In L. Joseph (Ed.). *Ferenczi apres Lacan*. Hermann Editeurs.

Jones, E. (1989). *A vida e a obra de Sigmund Freud* (Vol. 3). Imago.

Kahn, L. (2014). *Le psychanalyste apathique et le patient postmoderne*. Editions de l'Olivier.

Katz, C. S. (1996). Crianceria: o que é a criança. *Cadernos de Subjetividade*, *4*(n. esp.), 90–96.

Katz, C. S. (2009). Uma clínica de detalhes. In S. Ferenczi, *Coleção memória da psicanálise Sándor Ferenczi: a ética do cuidado* (Vol. 3). Duetto.

Knobloch, F. (1998). *O tempo do traumático*. Educ/Fapesp.

Koeppel, P. (1990). Lipps, reference freudienne. *Apertura - Collection de Recherche Psychanalytique*, *4*, 191–193.

Koritar, E. (2016). Relaxation in technique leading to new beginnings. *American Journal of Psychoanalysis*, *76*, 341–353.

Kristeva, J. (1995). The soul and the image. In *New maladies of the soul*. Columbia University Press.

Kupermann, D. (2003). *Ousar rir: humor, criação e psicanálise*. Civilização Brasileira.

Kupermann, D. (2008). *Presença sensível: cuidado e criação na clínica psicanalítica*. Civilização Brasileira.

Kupermann, D. (2010). A via sensível da elaboração. Caminhos da clínica psicanalítica. *Cadernos de Psicanálise*, *23*, 31–45.

Kupermann, D. (2014a). A maldição egípcia e as modalidades de intervenção clínica em Freud, Ferenczi e Winnicott. *Revista Brasileira de Psicanálise*, *48*(2), 47–58.

Kupermann, D. (2014b). *Transferências cruzadas: uma história da psicanálise e suas instituições*. Escuta.

Kupermann, D. (2017). *Estilos do cuidado: a psicanálise e o traumático*. Zagodoni.

Lacan, J. (1998). A coisa freudiana ou Sentido do retorno a Freud em psicanálise. In *Escritos* (V. Ribeiro, trad.). Jorge Zahar. (Original work published 1956)

Lacan, J. (2003). Proposição de 9 de outubro de 1967 sobre o psicanalista da Escola. In *Outros escritos* (V. Ribeiro, trad.). Jorge Zahar. (Original work published 1968)

Lacan, J. (2006a) Variations on the standard treatment. In *Ecrits. The first complete edition in English.* (B. Fink, trad). W.W. Norton & Company. (Original work published 1955)

Lacan, J. (2006b) On the subject who is finally in question. In *Ecrits. The first complete edition in english.* (B. Fink, trad.). W.W. Norton & Company. (Original work published 1966)

Landa, F. (1999). *Ensaio sobre a criação teórica em psicanálise: de Ferenczi a Nicolas Abraham e Maria Torok.* Unesp/Fapesp.

Laplanche, J. (1997). *Interpretar [com] Freud y otros ensayos.* Nueva Vision.

Levi, P. (1988). *É isto um homem?* Rocco.

Lugrin, Y. (2017). *Ferenczi sur le divan de freud: une analyse finie?* Campagne Premiere.

Maciel Jr. A., Barbosa, M. T., & Carvalho, M. S. (2018). A língua menor da ternura, confusão de língua e bilinguismo em psicanálise. In A. Maciel Jr. (Org.), *Trauma e ternura: a ética em Sándor Ferenczi.* 7 Letras.

Maia, M. S. (2004). *Extremos da alma: dor e trauma na atualidade e clínica psicanalítica.* Garamond.

Maia, M. S. (Org.). (2009). *Por uma ética do cuidado.* Garamond.

Mannoni, O. (1973). Eu sei, mas mesmo assim… In *Chaves para o imaginário.* Vozes.

Marcuse, H. (1998). A obsolescência da psicanálise. In *Cultura e sociedade* (L. M. Wolfgang, trad., Vol. 2). Paz e Terra.

Maryan, M. S. (2013). *La menagerie humaine.* Flammarion. Musee d'art et d'histoire du judaisme. Catálogo de exposição.

Mautner, A. V. (1996). Ferenczi: cultura e história. In Katz, C. S. (Org.), *Ferenczi: história, teoria, técnica*. 34/Formação Freudiana.

Mészáros, J. (2010). Building blocks toward contemporary trauma theory: Ferenczi's paradigm shift. *American Journal of Psychoanalysis, 70*, 328–340.

Mezan, R. (1993). Do auto-erotismo ao objeto: a simbolização segundo Ferenczi. *Percurso, 6*(10), 19–30.

Miller, J.-A. (2011). *Perspectivas dos escritos e outros escritos de Lacan: entre desejo e gozo*. Zahar.

Moraes, E. G., & Macedo, M. M. K. (2011). *Vivência de indiferença: do trauma ao ato-dor*. Casa do Psicólogo.

Osmo, A. (2016). *O testemunho de Maryan: limites e possibilidades na expressão do trauma*. (Master's thesis, Instituto de Psicologia da Universidade de São Paulo). doi:10.11606/D.47.2016.tde-21102016-153533

Osmo, A. (2018). *O testemunho de Maryan: limites e possibilidades na expressão do trauma*. Benjamin Editorial.

Osmo, A., & Kupermann, D. (2017). Trauma e testemunho: uma leitura de Maryan S. Maryan inspirada em Sándor Ferenczi. *Psicologia Clínica, 29*(3), 471–493. http://pepsic.bvsalud.org/scielo.php?script=sci_arttext&pid=S0103-56652017000300007&lng=pt&tlng=pt

Pankejeff, S. C. (1981). Mes souvenirs sur Sigmund Freud. In M. Gardiner (Org.). *L'Homme aux loups par ses psychanalystes et par lui-meme*. (L. Weibel, trad., p. 153–171). Gallimard.

Pigman, G. W. (1995). Freud e a história da empatia. *Livro Anual de Psicanálise, 11*, 123–142.

Pimentel, P. K. A., & Coelho Jr., N. (2009). Algumas considerações sobre o uso da empatia em casos e situações limite. *Psicologia Clínica, 21*(2), 301–314. http://dx.doi.org/10.1590/S0103-56652009000200004

Pinheiro, T. (1995). *Ferenczi: do grito a palavra*. Jorge Zahar; Editora UFRJ.

Pinheiro, T. (2016). *Ferenczi*. Casa do Psicólogo.

Prado de Oliveira, L. R. (2011). *Sándor Ferenczi. La psychanalyse autrement*. Armand Colin.

Prado de Oliveira, L. R. (2012). *O sentido da amizade em Ferenczi: uma contribuição a clínica psicanalítica*. Uape.

Rachman, A. (1999). Ferenczi's Rise and Fall from "Analytic Grace": The Ferenczi Renaissance Revisited. *Group*, *23*(3/4), 103–119. http://www.jstor.org/stable/41718912

Rank, O. (1929). *The trauma of birth*. Dover Edition. (Original work published 1924)

Reis, E. S., & Gondar, J. (2017). *Com Ferenczi: clínica, subjetivação, política*. 7 Letras.

Robert, P. F. P. (2015). *Da transferência negativa a destrutividade: percursos da clínica psicanalítica*. (Doctoral dissertation, Instituto de Psicologia da Universidade de São Paulo). doi:10.11606/T.47.2015.tde-13072015-121208

Robert, P. P., & Kupermann, D. (2012). Dor e resistência na clínica psicanalítica. O manejo das transferências negativas em Freud. *Cadernos de Psicanálise*, *34*(26), 37–49. http://pepsic.bvsalud.org/scielo.php?script=sci_arttext&pid=S1413-62952012000100004&lng=pt&tlng=pt

Robert, P. P., & Kupermann, D. (2015). Suportar o ódio, suportar o próprio ódio: os casos R.N., S.I. e os limites na clínica de Ferenczi. *Cadernos de Psicanálise*, *37*(33), 175–193. http://pepsic.bvsalud.org/scielo.php?script=sci_arttext&pid=S1413-62952015000200009&lng=pt&tlng=pt

Rocha, Z. (2011). A ontologia heideggeriana do cuidado e suas ressonâncias clínicas. *Síntese – Revista de Filosofia*, *38*(120), 71–90.

Rocha, Z. (2013). Para uma clínica psicanalítica do cuidado. *Tempo Psicanalítico*, 45(2), 453–471.

Rozenthal, E. (2014). *O ser no gerúndio: corpo e sensibilidade na psicanálise*. Companhia de Freud.

Rudnytsky, P. (1996). Introduction: Ferenczi's turn in psychoanalysis. In P. Rudnytsky, A. Bokay & P. Giampieri-Deutsch (Eds.). *Ferenczi's turn in psuchoanalysis*. New York University Press.

Rudnytsky, P. (2015). The other side of the story: Severn on Ferenczi and mutual analysis. In A. Harris & S. Kuchuck (Eds.). *The legacy of Sándor Ferenczi: from ghost to ancestor*. Routledge.

Sabourin, P. (1988). *Ferenczi - paladino e grão-vizir secreto*. Martins Fontes.

Schneider, M. (1994). *Afeto e linguagem nos primeiros escritos de Freud*. Escuta.

Soreanu, R. (2018). *Working-through collective wounds*. Palgrave Macmillan.

Stevens, A. (1992). La fin de la cure analytique pour Ferenczi. *Le Coq-Heron*, (125), 11–14.

Tardits, A. (2009). "Le temps de Ferenczi doit encore venir" (Lou Andreas-Salome): La question de la formation. In L. Joseph (Ed.). *Ferenczi apres Lacan*. Hermann Editeurs.

Torok, M. (1995). Doença do luto e fantasia do cadáver saboroso. In N. Abraham & M. Torok, *A casca e o núcleo*. Escuta.

Vernant, J-P. (1991). Death in the eyes: Gorgo, figure of the other. In *Mortals and immortals — Collected essays*. Princeton University Press.

Verztman, J. S. (2002). O observador do mundo: a noção de clivagem em Ferenczi. *Agora: Estudos em Teoria Psicanalítica*, 5(1), 59–78. https://dx.doi.org/10.1590/S1516-14982002000100005

Vieira, B. A. (2017). *A empatia em Freud e em Ferenczi: em busca de uma ferramenta para a clínica psicanalítica* (Master's thesis, Instituto de Psicologia da Universidade de São Paulo). doi:10.11606/D.47.2017.tde-01092017-094544

Vitorello, D. M. (2015). *Autenticidade: o psicanalista entre Ferenczi e Lacan.* (Doctoral dissertation, Instituto de Psicologia da Universidade de São Paulo). doi: 10.11606/T.47.2015.tde-06082015-163453

Wajcman, G. (2013). Help! In *Maryan. La menagerie humanine* (p. 83–93, catalogue d'exposition). Flammarion. Musee d'art et d'histoire du judaisme.

Winnicott, D. W. (1960). Distorção do ego em termos de verdadeiro e falso *self.* In *O ambiente e os processos de maturação: estudos sobre a teoria do desenvolvimento emocional.* Artes Médicas.

Winnicott, D. W. (2000a). Desenvolvimento emocional primitivo. In *Da pediatria a psicanálise: obras escolhidas.* Imago. (Original work published 1945)

Winnicott, D. W. (2000b). Psicoses e cuidados maternos. In *Da pediatria a psicanálise: obras escolhidas* (D. Bogomoletz, trad.). Imago. (Original work published 1952)

Winnicott, D. W. (2000c). Aspectos clínicos e metapsicológicos da regressão no contexto psicanalítico. In *Da pediatria a psicanálise: obras escolhidas* (D. Bogomoletz, trad., p. 374–392). Imago. (Original work published 1954)

Winnicott, D. W. (2000d). *O brincar & a realidade.* Imago. (Original work published 1975)

Winnicott, D. W. (2018). Postscript: D.W.W. on D.W.W. In C. Winnicott & R. Shepherd, *Psycho-analytic explorations* (p. 569–584). Routledge. (Original work published 1967)

Yovel, Y. (1993) *Espinosa e outros hereges.* Casa da Moeda.

GRÁFICA PAYM
Tel. [11] 4392-3344
paym@graficapaym.com.br